Cambridge Elements

Elements in Cognitive Linguistics
edited by
Sarah Duffy
Northumbria University
Nick Riches
Newcastle University

COMPUTATIONAL CONSTRUCTION GRAMMAR

A Usage-Based Approach

Jonathan Dunn
University of Illinois Urbana-Champaign

Shaftesbury Road, Cambridge CB2 8EA, United Kingdom

One Liberty Plaza, 20th Floor, New York, NY 10006, USA

477 Williamstown Road, Port Melbourne, VIC 3207, Australia

314–321, 3rd Floor, Plot 3, Splendor Forum, Jasola District Centre, New Delhi – 110025, India

103 Penang Road, #05–06/07, Visioncrest Commercial, Singapore 238467

Cambridge University Press is part of Cambridge University Press & Assessment, a department of the University of Cambridge.

We share the University's mission to contribute to society through the pursuit of education, learning and research at the highest international levels of excellence.

www.cambridge.org
Information on this title: www.cambridge.org/9781009507608

DOI: 10.1017/9781009233743

When citing this work, please include a reference to the DOI 10.1017/9781009233743

First published 2024

A catalogue record for this publication is available from the British Library.

ISBN 978-1-009-50760-8 Hardback
ISBN 978-1-009-23376-7 Paperback
ISSN 2633-3325 (online)
ISSN 2633-3317 (print)

Additional resources for this publication at http://www.cambridge.org/Dunn

Computational Construction Grammar

A Usage-Based Approach

Elements in Cognitive Linguistics

DOI: 10.1017/9781009233743
First published online: June 2024

Jonathan Dunn
University of Illinois Urbana-Champaign

Author for correspondence: Jonathan Dunn, jedunn@illinois.edu

Abstract: This Element introduces a usage-based computational approach to Construction Grammar that draws on techniques from natural language processing and unsupervised machine learning. This work explores how to represent constructions, how to learn constructions from a corpus, and how to arrange the constructions in a grammar as a network. From a theoretical perspective, this Element examines how construction grammars emerge from usage alone as complex systems, with slot-constraints learned at the same time that constructions are learned. From a practical perspective, this work is accompanied by a Python package which enables linguists to incorporate construction grammars into their own corpus-based work. The computational experiments in this Element are important for testing the learnability, variability, and confirmability of Construction Grammar as a theory of language. All code examples will leverage the cloud computing platform Code Ocean to guide readers through implementation of these algorithms.

Keywords: Computational syntax, usage-based grammar, Construction Grammar, cognitive grammar, cognitive linguistics

JEL classifications: A12, B34, C56, D78, E90

ISBNs: 9781009507608 (HB), 9781009233767 (PB), 9781009233743 (OC)
ISSNs: 2633-3325 (online), 2633-3317 (print)

Contents

1 Representing Constructions

This Element formulates an unsupervised computational approach to Construction Grammar (CxG). From a scientific perspective, this work provides a computational theory of human language that ranges from category formation to the emergence of structure given exposure to usage. From a practical perspective, it provides a tool for large-scale corpus analysis, useful even for linguists who are not concerned with the specific hypotheses behind CxG.

What exactly is *Computational Construction Grammar*? First, CxG itself is an approach to grammar based on constructions: symbolic mappings between form and meaning at different levels of abstraction (Goldberg, 1995, 2006; Langacker, 2008). When we say that constructions exist at different levels of abstraction, this means that some are quite item specific (like *give X a hand*) and others are quite schematic (like *the X'er the Y'er*). In more formal terms, constructions are constraint-based representations, a series of *slots*, each of which is defined by a specific *slot-filler*. These slot-fillers are constraints; for example, a schematic construction might have a syntactic slot-filler like NOUN PHRASE or an idiomatic construction might have a lexical slot-filler like "hand." Thus, the level of abstraction depends on the kinds of constraints which a construction contains.[1] Part of learning constructions is learning the categories or concepts available for formulating such slot-constraints. Because constructions are meaningful, slot-constraints can be semantic in nature and there is no strict separation between purely schematic (i.e., syntactic) and purely meaningful representations: Usage-based slot-constraints combine form and meaning.

Computational CxG is a fully replicable and falsifiable implementation of CxG that makes testable predictions about the grammars which would emerge given certain sets of exposure (i.e., training corpora). From a linguistic perspective, computational CxG is a *discovery-device grammar*, a mapping between learning mechanisms and specific learned representations (Goldsmith, 2015). This is especially important for CxG, which views language not as a set of innate structures but rather as a set of general learning mechanisms which produce grammatical representations given exposure to previous production. From a computational perspective, this discovery-device grammar is drawn from unsupervised machine learning. There is a dual focus in this Element on the theoretical properties of CxG and on the specific computational methods used for simulating and experimenting with these theoretical properties.

[1] Note that we will use the term *slot* even if only a single lexical item can occupy that position. This is because lexical items are one type of BASIC CONSTRUCTION so that, even if a slot cannot be filled by multiple items, it can still be viewed as a constraint on the more lexical side of the lexico-grammatical continuum.

The goal is to provide a replicable and falsifiable theory of CxG in the form of a computational model. The first question involves the **learnability** of representations: To what degree can grammatical generalizations emerge from usage with minimal starting assumptions? Linguistic theory has often assumed with no evidence that usage alone is not sufficient to make generalizations. This Element probes just how much structure can be learned from usage alone. Knowledge-based approaches, which rely on hand-crafted representations of constructions that are based on the introspections of trained linguists, are unable to answer questions about learnability because they depend entirely on the introspections of those who already possess linguistic knowledge.

The second question involves the **variability** of representations: What are the sources of difference in grammar and in usage across individuals, across registers, and across populations? Variation is a core phenomenon of language. Recent computational studies have further illustrated how pervasive (Dunn & Nini, 2021) and how predictable (Dunn, 2018a) such syntactic variation is. This Element shows how grammatical structures differ across register and also how constructions and construction grammars become more complex given increased exposure: Structure accumulates as existing constructions enable the discovery of more complex constructions which depend on them.

The third question involves the **confirmability** of representations: To what degree are claims about the meaning or interpretation of constructions stable and reproducible? Because cognitive linguistics focuses heavily on meaning, introspections are made about everything from metaphoricity (Dunn, 2010) to the implications of idiomatic utterances in slightly different forms (Dunn, 2013). Intuitions about meaning are an essential piece of linguistic methodology. But how do we test the robustness of those intuitions when every practitioner knows the difficulty of operationalizing semantic concepts? The approach in this work is to first learn constructions without reference to a linguist's intuitions about meaning and then to analyze those constructions using introspection. This approach removes the circularity involved in both hypothesizing and testing constructions using the same data source (our own introspections).

For these reasons, we mean by *Computational Construction Grammar* a theory of language implemented as a computational model which makes predictions about the grammar of constructions and their relationships to one another given exposure to the unelicited usage found in a corpus (cf., Wible & Tsao, 2010, 2020). From this perspective, Computational Construction Grammar is not a collection of manual annotations of specific construction types (although it provides such a *constructicon* as output). Rather, it is an implemented theory of the role of exposure in the emergence of both linguistic

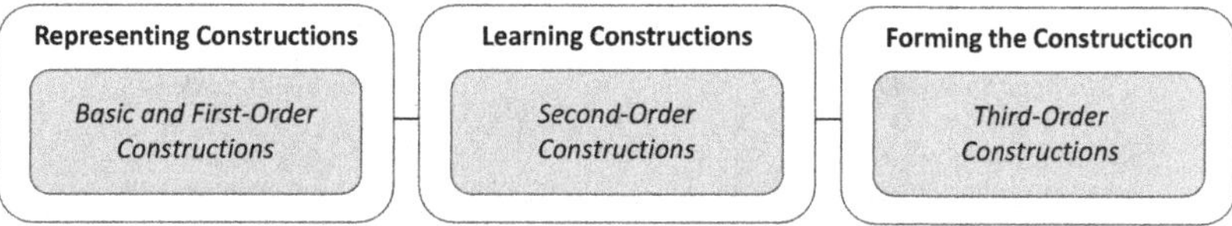

Figure 1 Structure of this Element. *Basic Constructions* are the categories which form slot-constraints; *First-Order Constructions* are chunks or sequences of slot-constraints; *Second-Order Constructions* instead use existing first-order constructions as slot-constraints; and *Third-Order Constructions* are larger families containing multiple related constructions.

categories and the structures which depend on them, of the range of possible grammars, and of the sources and manifestations of grammatical variation.

The approach to computational CxG taken here is based on the underlying idea that constructions are learned starting with surface-level chunks, which are then increasingly generalized given distributional information to form more and more abstract representations. This is implemented in the form of (i) scaffolded structure in which the same algorithm is applied to new input together with its own previous outputs (cf., Section 2.7) and (ii) higher-order constructions which use first-order chunks as slot-constraints (cf., Section 2.6). From a semantic perspective, this is informed by the *Principle of No Synonymy* (Goldberg, 1995) in which each entrenched construction will acquire a unique meaning, whether that is semantic meaning (propositional), pragmatic meaning (non-propositional), or social meaning (an externally conditioned variable). Given the possibility of differences in social meaning (Dunn, 2018a), this is better formulated as the *Principle of No Equivalence* (Leclercq & Morin, 2023). Regardless of the name, however, the idea is that the entrenchment of unique forms implies the unique meaning of these forms on some level. In other words, these constructions are form–meaning mappings, with the caveat that (i) social meaning is a kind of meaning and (ii) representing the semantics for each construction computationally remains a problem for future work.

Recent work in Fluid Construction Grammar (FCG: Beuls & Van Eecke, 2023; Doumen, Beuls, & Van Eecke, 2023; Nevens et al., 2022) provides an alternate approach to CxG which still satisfies our core criteria of learnability, variability, and confirmability. This recent work focuses instead on the idea that the learning process is guided by *intention reading*, either by situating the learning process within embodied agents or by including semantic annotations of corpora (thus, starting with a set of basic semantic primitives). The starting assumption, in other words, is that the language learner is able to determine the meaning of each utterance by its specific context.[2]

[2] If this were entirely true, of course, humans would not need language in the first place.

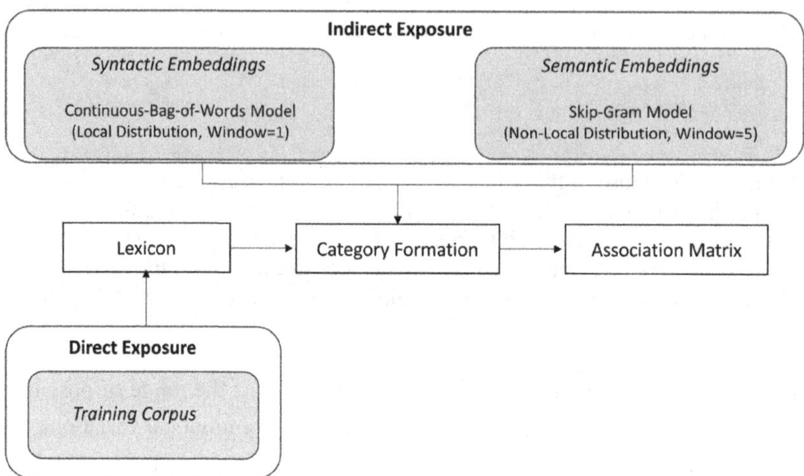

Figure 2 Learning an emerging ontology of slot-constraints (acquiring linguistic knowledge and world knowledge)

This recent work in FCG has been ground-breaking in a number of areas that have been weaknesses of approaches which depend on large background corpora: The exposure is specific to the individual learner and is grounded within meaningful interactions. By contrast, approaches based on large corpora necessarily work with aggregated exposure (with some exceptions like Dunn & Nini, 2021) and in doing so remove that exposure from individual communicative situations. The main difference in these frameworks is the use of background data as *indirect exposure*, as shown in Figure 2. By viewing the corpus as a store of linguistic experience we can learn aggregated representations like word embeddings or association measures. But doing this necessarily abstracts away from the full communicative situation involved with each utterance. On the other hand, acquiring linguistic knowledge necessarily requires such abstraction.

The first section of this Element, Representing Constructions, presents a computational and usage-based approach to representing constructions, as outlined in Figure 2. These representations are *computational* because they exist as fully implemented data structures. And they are *usage based* because they are learned in a data-driven manner from actual corpora. These constructional representations include both slot-constraints (like semantic domains or syntactic categories) as well as hierarchical relationships between slots.

The second section, Learning Constructions, focuses on the mechanisms of entrenchment and emergence in which particular constructions become a part of the grammar and are then abstracted away from specific lexical phrases.

This is a form of discovery-device grammar which requires both (i) a method for searching through potential constructions and (ii) a measure of quality for potential grammars. This section introduces the idea of *second-order* constructions, in which slot-constraints are satisfied by existing constructions. It also introduces the idea of *scaffolded structure*, in which representations grow more complex over new iterations of exposure as the current constructicon enables the emergence of more complex constructions.

The third section, Forming the Constructicon, explores the emergent properties of a grammar as a network of constructions rather than a set of isolated representations. This begins with a look at both the growth of the constructicon and at change in the constructicon as constructions are forgotten. We then use relationships between constructions to create a network that contains families of related constructions. This leads to an examination of emergent relationships between slot-constraints, in which we observe coercion between basic-level categories when they appear in the same construction.

We begin this first section by introducing the basic descriptions that will be used to notate constructions, along with the computational challenges involved in learning these representations (Section 1.1). We then frame the problem of the emergence of linguistic structure as an unsupervised learning problem (Section 1.2), which involves using distribution to measure relationships between words (Section 1.3) in order to group them into categories that can be used to formulate slot-constraints (Section 1.4). We then consider *attraction*, or the relationship between a slot-filler and a slot-constraint (Section 1.5). This leads us to the related problem of finding relationships between slots within a construction (Section 1.6). We end by considering the relationship between computational and cognitive representations, the first step in relating this approach to the non-computational literature (Section 1.7).

An important part of this work is that all aspects of the analysis are available in a Python implementation. First, a Python package is available for both learning and then using construction grammars for actual problems in linguistic analysis.[3] Second, the Element is accompanied by a containerized notebook which contains the data and the environment necessary to undertake working analyses using the Python package.[4] Third, the supplementary materials contain detailed information for each of the register-specific grammars of English that are discussed here.[5]

[3] www.github.com/jonathandunn/c2xg.
[4] https://doi.org/10.24433/CO.9944630.v1.
[5] https://doi.org/10.17605/OSF.IO/SA6R3.

1.1 Constructions as Slot-Constraints

This section focuses on how to represent constructions within an unsupervised computational framework. A construction is a sequence of SLOTS, each of which is defined using a SLOT-CONSTRAINT. For consistency, even a position which allows only a single filler is called a slot: a slot with an idiomatic lexical constraint. We notate constructions as in (1), a simple convention that allows us to use the same notation here and in the Python implementation. In this notation, the brackets indicate the boundaries of the construction and the dashes indicate the boundaries between slots within the construction (thus, this example has four slots). The problem of learning the boundaries of constructions and of slots is a matter of SEGMENTATION that is explored further in Section 2.2.

(1) [SYN: NP – SEM: <*transfer*> – SYN: NP – SYN: NP]

Each slot is described using the constraints which define it. These constraints are written using two labels: First, the type of representation is given in small caps: LEX refers to lexical representations, SYN to syntactic representations, and SEM to semantic. Within each type of representation, the SLOT-FILLER is the particular category used to define the contents of that slot. For example, the syntactic constraint NP refers to a noun phrase and the semantic constraint <*transfer*> refers to any item from that semantic domain. These are introspection-based examples as we have not yet developed the unsupervised ontology of slot-constraints which, in later sections, will be used to formulate constructions.

The problem of learning a discrete set of constraints for a given language is a matter of CATEGORY FORMATION, explored further in Sections 1.3 and 1.4. Given previous work in cognitive linguistics we would expect these categories to have a prototype structure and to differ across languages (Taylor, 2004). This means, then, that the first step in learning a grammar is to model category formation and the emergence of concepts. We refer to the categories with which slot-constraints are defined as BASIC CONSTRUCTIONS, the primitive mappings between form and meaning. Here we approach that problem using unsupervised machine learning applied to large unannotated corpora. Categories, like constructions themselves, emerge given exposure to usage.

The difference between syntactic and semantic categories here is not absolute: The semantic constraints reflect mostly non-syntactic information but the syntactic constraints will necessarily include semantic information. The basic distinction reflects the two different approaches used to observe the distribution of words: Syntactic constraints rely on local observations (embeddings trained to predict each word given its immediately surrounding context) and semantic constraints on non-local observations (embeddings trained to use each word to predict the content words which occur within a surrounding window).

The problem of selecting a set of slot-constraints for each potential construction is explored further in Sections 2.3 and 2.4. Construction grammars present a more difficult search problem than other types of grammars because we must search across types of constraints (like syntactic vs. semantic) as well as specific slot-fillers (like different semantic domains). This creates a larger *hypothesis space* of potential grammars. An important part of CxG as a theory of human language is that constructions are hypothesized to vary in their level of abstractness (e.g., idiomatic constructions) and to include meaning-based constraints (e.g., semantic domains). Both of these attributes make searching more difficult because we must consider more POTENTIAL CONSTRUCTIONS. From a usage-based perspective, the only way to know which potential constructions have become entrenched is to observe the usage of a community of speaker-hearers, as contained in a corpus.

What exactly is a potential construction? Consider the construction in (2), which differs from (1) in that the final slot-constraint is limited to the lexical item *a hand*. The utterance in (3) is a token or example of the construction in (2), but it is also a token of the construction in (1). Thus, this utterance is described by two separate constructions in the grammar. In fact, we could formulate a large number of alternate constructions which would capture most of the same sets of utterances. We consider the relationship between grammar complexity and the number of idiomatic constructions in Section 2.7 and the problem of similarity networks between constructions in Sections 3.3 and 3.4. The point here is that the search for constructions is made more difficult by these overlapping constructional representations.

(2) [SYN: NP – SEM: *<transfer>* – SYN: NP – LEX: *a hand*]

(3) The neighbor gave us a hand.

A closely related problem is the matter of implicit relationships between slot-constraints. For example, in (1) the main verb is represented using a semantic constraint which, in fact, does not specify that only verbs can occupy that position. However, given the context of a double object argument structure, in practice only verbs would be observed occupying that central slot in the construction. This kind of implicit influence between slot-constraints, an emergent property of constructions, in considered further in Section 3.5.

The combination of idiomatic constructions, meaning-based slot-constraints, and implicit relationships between slots all serve to make the problem of learnability in CxG more difficult than in other syntactic paradigms. As we will

Table 1 List of corpora used in this Element.

Name and abbreviation		Description	Words
Project Gutenberg [a]	PG	Books from 1850 to 1919	529 mil
Wikipedia [b]	WK	Non-fiction articles	138 mil
European Parliament [c]	EU	Speeches in proceedings	56 mil
News comments [d]	NC	Comments on newspaper articles	139 mil
Product reviews [e]	PR	Reviews from Amazon.com	170 mil
Open subtitles [f]	OS	Dialogue from movies and TV	198 mil
Blogs [g]	BL	Web-crawled blog posts	111 mil
Tweets [h]	TW	Tweets from six countries	660 mil
		Size used for semantic domains	**2.0 bil**

[a] Rae, Potapenko, Jayakumar, and Lillicrap (2019)
[b] Ortman (2018)
[c] Tiedemann (2012)
[d] Kesarwani (2018)
[e] Zhang, Zhao, and LeCun (2015)
[f] Lison and Tiedemann (2016)
[g] Schler et al. (2006)
[h] Dunn (2020)

see, however, it remains possible to learn a constructicon from observed usage while making no starting assumptions about the types of structures the grammar contains. This problem is revisited in the discussion of parsing constructions in Section 2.5.

The list of corpora used in this work is given in Table 1. For learning embeddings (Section 1.3), we use the entire corpus of approximately 2 billion words; for all other experiments, we use a random subset from each source as described in the specific sections. These corpora provide a range of written registers that we will treat as the production to which a learner is exposed.

1.2 Lexical Constraints

In this and the next sections we focus on the problem of learning slot-constraints from usage, starting here with lexical constraints. The first challenge for learning the grammar of a particular language is to determine the ontology of slot-fillers within each type of constraint. Rather than formulate particular slot-constraints by hand as a set of syntactic and semantic primitives, our grammar instead specifies the process by which specific categories emerge given exposure to usage. These BASIC CONSTRUCTIONS, the categories of a language, are partly based on meaning and partly on form, resulting in constructions which function as mappings between form and meaning.

Lexical constraints are the first and the simplest types of slot-constraints, in the sense that syntactic and semantic constraints are based on categories of lexical items. Thus, lexical constraints come first, as explored further in models of scaffolded structure in Section 2.7. While simpler, there are still two problems that need to be solved: segmentation (what counts as a word) and selection (which words are learned and belong in the lexicon).

In the first case, defining a word, we analyze word-forms using white space, so that the utterance in (4) contains the lower-cased word-forms listed in (5). Given the inflectional morphology of English, we know that *message* is the singular form, thus part of the same paradigm as the plural form *messages*. In many cases we want to generalize across particular morphological forms within the same paradigm. However, there are some item-specific constructions which are sensitive to particular word-forms: For example, (6) has an interpretation distinct from that of (4). Thus, we want to restrict some constraints to specific word-forms, while we want others to generalize across paradigms.

(4) I got the message.

(5) [*i, got, message, the*]

(6) I got the messages.

From a practical perspective, larger word classes will be captured by the distributional constraints described in the next section. For example, in the case of (4), both the singular and plural could be described as members of a semantic domain for communication objects (*email, letter, voicemail*, etc). We use character-based embeddings, which improve the representation of morphological information, during category formation (Section 1.4). The expansion of computational CxG to include constructional morphology remains a problem for future work.

$$\text{NPMI}(x,y) = \left[\ln \frac{p(x,y)}{p(x) * p(y)}\right] \Big/ -\ln p(x,y) \qquad (1)$$

As part of learning the vocabulary of lexical constraints, we allow for multi-word expressions using pointwise mutual information (PMI) as a measure of association (Church & Hanks, 1990). This means that lexical phrases such as *public domain* or *ronald reagan* or *st louis* can be treated as a single slot-filler while maintaining an entirely unsupervised framework. Here we use a normalized variant, the NPMI, which restricts values to between -1 and 1 (Bouma, 2009). Given that we learn grammars across different amounts of exposure, this

Table 2 Examples of lexical constructions (PG).

Names	Places	Words with spaces	Noun phrases
monte cristo	san francisco	vice versa	lemon juice
da vinci	monte carlo	per cent	frying pan
van buren	corpus christi	habeas corpus	nineteenth century
genghis khan	new york	don t	protective tariff
anglo saxon	champs elysees	bas reliefs	coral reefs

normalization allows us to maintain a similar threshold across the total number of words observed. This NPMI is shown in Equation (1), with the first portion indicating the standard PMI, which is then normalized through dividing by the negative log of the probability that x and y occur together.

Some examples of multi-word phrases that are discovered using the NPMI are shown in Table 2, derived from 10 million words from the Project Gutenberg corpus with a threshold of 0.75. The first column represents proper names, of people and groups of people. The second column represents places. The third column represents words which include a space in the orthography, mostly borrowings but also, given our pre-processing, contractions such as *don t*. The final column represents noun phrases which occur together so regularly that they have become a single item. For the purposes of the grammar, these phrases are added to the lexicon and treated as a single word.

1.3 Distributional Constraints

This section presents two types of slot-constraints which are formulated using word embeddings and, at a basic level, capture distributional information from a background corpus. The basic approach here is to formulate slot-constraints within an embedding space and then to view the centroid of each slot-filler as its prototype or exemplar. We use two distinct embedding spaces to focus on two distinct pieces of linguistic information. In the first case, we want more syntactic constraints (SYN) to capture local co-occurrence information. For example, in the phrase *I want to X*, the slot represented by X is almost certainly a verb in the infinitive form. In the second case, we want more semantic constraints (SEM) to capture non-local co-occurrence information. For example, a phrasal verb like *pop out* is more likely to occur along with contexts like *I didn't mean to say it* or *it fell apart*. This section introduces and evaluates these distributional constraints from a computational perspective.

We want to avoid building specific structures into the model: For example, if we assume a distinction between *noun* and *verb*, we have to support that assumption with a further assumption about a genetic predisposition toward this category system in order to justify hard-coding them into our ontology. We take a different approach in which the formation of linguistic categories follows from the general language learning framework. Thus, our syntactic and semantic primitives are entirely unsupervised, learned only from the observed distribution of words in the background corpus. The power of distributional representations is that they create a network of word-level relationships: The more vocabulary the learner has observed, the more links there are in this network. Denser networks, in turn, lead to more robust categories.

We model the distribution of words in a corpus using character-based word embeddings within the fastText framework (Grave et al., 2018). For syntactic categories we use a continuous-bag-of-words model (CBOW: Mikolov, Chen, et al. (2013)) and for semantic categories a skip-gram model (SG: Mikolov, Sutskever, et al. (2013)), both trained using negative sampling. These word embeddings were originally developed in the context of language modeling, in which the goal is to predict which word comes next as we move through a corpus. Word embeddings are also called *dense representations* because they represent a word as a fixed-length numerical vector with no sparse elements. A detailed analysis of these embeddings is available elsewhere (Dunn, 2022b). From our perspective here, the purpose of dense word representations is to maintain an isomorphic relationship between (i) the network of words in the set of embeddings (the model) and (ii) the lexicon of a speaker of the language (the lexical semantics that is being modeled). This means that the semantic relationships which make *road* and *street* similar for speakers should be mirrored in the relationship between their word vectors, as measured, for example, using cosine similarity.

Drawing on the language modeling task, these word embeddings are trained using a logistic regression classifier in which each word in the vocabulary is an observation. The number of features in the classifier corresponds to the dimensionality of the embeddings: For example, we use 100-dimensional embeddings, which means that each word is represented by 100 feature weights. During training, these weights are used to predict which words occur together and, after training, they are exported as the embeddings or word vectors.

The distinction between CBOW and SG embeddings has to do with the prediction task used during training. For syntactic constraints we use the CBOW task with a context window of 1. For each word in the corpus, the classifier is trained to predict the target word (D in Figure 3) given the context words (C and E in

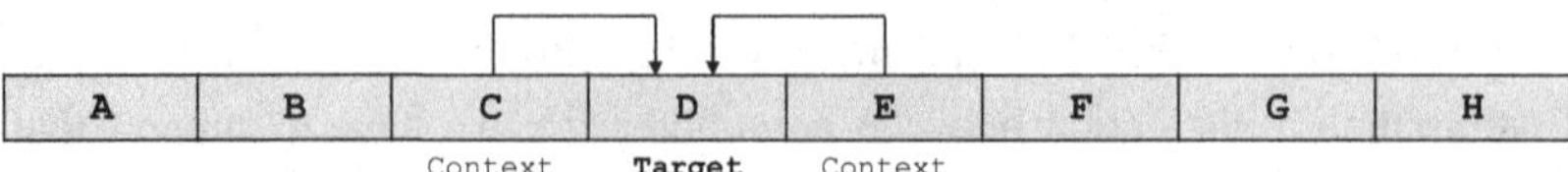

Figure 3 Optimization task for the CBOW algorithm (syntactic constraints).

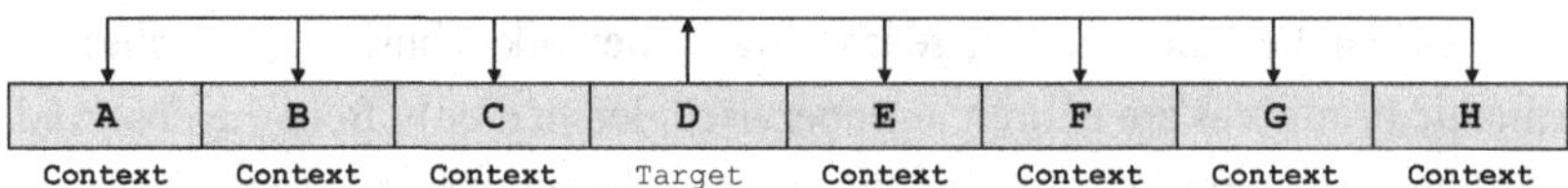

Figure 4 Optimization task for the SG algorithm (semantic constraints).

the figure). The window size of 1 means that at most two words will be used for prediction. Thus, for CBOW, the adjacent context predicts the target word (thus, the target is shown in bold). This algorithm is suitable for finding more schematic or syntactic constraints because it is largely focused on how words are arranged within a sequence. For example, in the phrase *I want to X a book*, the predicted embedding for *X* would be drawn from the embeddings for *I want to* on the left and *a book* on the right. These embeddings thus represent joint form–meaning patterns: options here would be *read, write, edit* but not *blue, the, dog*, capturing both part-of-speech and semantic information.

For the SG embeddings, on the other hand, the prediction task during training uses the target word to predict the context words, as shown in Figure 4. Here we use the SG task with a context window of 5, which means that the classifier is trying to predict up to five words in each direction from the target (thus, the context slots are shown in bold). For example, in *X* above in *I want to X a book* is *read*, these embeddings focus on words which typically belong to the same semantic script. We might expect *page, topic, study* to be close to *read* in this embedding space, but not *run, limp, walk*. In this sense, the SG algorithm is suitable for finding more meaning-based constraints because it is largely focused on how words occur within a given frame or script regardless of the syntactic arrangement of those words.

The main distinction, then, is that CBOW with a small window size is focused on the arrangement of words, while SG with a large window size is focused on the content of words. The boundary between purely syntactic and purely semantic constraints is not always clear, one of the starting observations for work in CxG. Given the preceding discussion, SYN constraints will certainly contain some semantic information, although it is less likely that SEM constraints are limited to a single part of speech. The labels SYN and SEM were chosen as a convenient shorthand for these two facets of distributional information. Another way to view the distinction between types of slot-constraints is the scope of each slot-filler: LEX constraints are fixed to one item per category, SEM constraints have between ten and fifty items per category, and SYN constraints are more unspecified with dozens or hundreds of items per category. In other words, syntactic constraints leave slots only partially filled because they are based on schematic rather than meaning-based information.[6]

These word embeddings are thus a type of self-supervised language model which is trained to predict held-out words from the corpus (i.e., each target word becomes a held-out prediction in the CBOW task). The difference between them is that the syntactic word vectors are optimized to predict local adjacent contexts and the semantic word vectors are optimized to predict the larger context window (e.g., that *street* and *road* both occur with *cross* or *traffic*). The average sentences in our corpora range from twenty-six to twenty-seven words long (Project Gutenberg and the European Parliament) to fifteen to sixteen words long (tweets and subtitles). The semantic word vectors thus capture a larger sub-portion of each sentence, while the syntactic word vectors observe only adjacent context.

$$Target \cdot Context = T_1C_1 + T_2C_2 + T_3C_3 \ldots T_nC_n \tag{2}$$

These embeddings use the negative sampling approach to training, in which the actual context words are classified against n random samples drawn from the vocabulary (here, $n = 100$). Thus, the probability of the actual context should be higher than the probability of the randomly sampled context: in CBOW, $p(target|context)$ versus $p(random|context)$. In other words, the probability of the actually observed target word should be higher given the context than the probability of the randomly sampled word it is compared with. The notion of probability in this case is replaced with the dot product of the word vectors. Thus, as shown in Equation (3), the probability of the target given the context word is calculated as the elementwise multiplication of the two current word vectors (i.e., their dot product). During training the model weights (i.e., the word vectors) are gradually updated to maximize the overall prediction accuracy.

$$\sigma(p) = \frac{1}{1 + e^{-p}} \tag{3}$$

Logistic regression is so named because it depends on the logistic or sigmoid function to make predictions. The dot product used in Equation (3) is scalar,

[6] Ideally, constructions would also allow unfilled slots as a way of capturing non-contiguous constructions. Such unfilled slots are not directly included in this Element (although second-order constructions in Section 2.6 have some properties of non-contiguous constructions). This remains a challenge for future work and is most likely to be addressed by including null or meaningless slot-constraints as an additional level of representation.

but it is not a probability. Here, the sigmoid function is used to convert this into a probability with values further away from the midpoint. After passing the dot product through the sigmoid function, the prediction of real versus random contexts falls between 0 and 1, with the goal during training of maximizing the probability of the actual context. For the SG task, the prediction of each context word is assumed to be independent of the other context words for simplicity, so that it remains a binary classification problem.

To summarize, the CBOW algorithm optimizes word vectors to predict each target word given the immediately adjacent context words. The SG algorithm optimizes word vectors to predict each context word in a bidirectional five-word window given the target word. The model weights are trained using logistic regression to predict each target position in the training corpus, with the dot product standing in for probability. After training, the model weights are used to represent each word. We use the fastText-based character variant for these word vectors, which operates by dividing each word into character n-grams (thus, *street* becomes *stre* + *tree* + *reet*), with the final word vector a simple sum of each component subword n-gram. This approach provides additional flexibility in computing a word vector for those words which were not observed in the training corpus (out-of-vocabulary words).

A recurring issue with word embeddings is that they are somewhat unstable (Burdick, Kummerfeld, & Mihalcea, 2021; Hellrich, Kampe, & Hahn, 2019). This means that we could observe potentially wide variation in word vectors given similar training data across multiple iterations. One reason is that the training process depends on randomly sampled negative examples, so that we can improve stability by using a relatively large *n* (Levy, Goldberg, & Dagan, 2015). We can evaluate the stability of an embedding model by shuffling a corpus and retraining multiple times under the same conditions. Here we shuffle and retrain both the CBOW and SG models twice each using the corpus described in Table 1. The similarity of individual words across embeddings can be measured by retrieving the *k* nearest neighbors in both sets of embeddings and quantifying the overlap: 100 percent overlap would indicate complete agreement but a lower score like 25 percent would indicate minimal overlap.

The violin plot in Figure 5 shows the distribution of nearest neighbor overlaps for the reshuffled and retrained CBOW embeddings: This represents agreement from the same model trained on the same corpus shuffled so that it is observed in a different order. The y-axis represents the percent of overlap, with higher values indicating higher stability. The x-axis represents the lexicon binned into ages of acquisition, taken from participant-based ratings in Kuperman, Stadthagen-Gonzalez, and Brysbaert (2012). The width of each

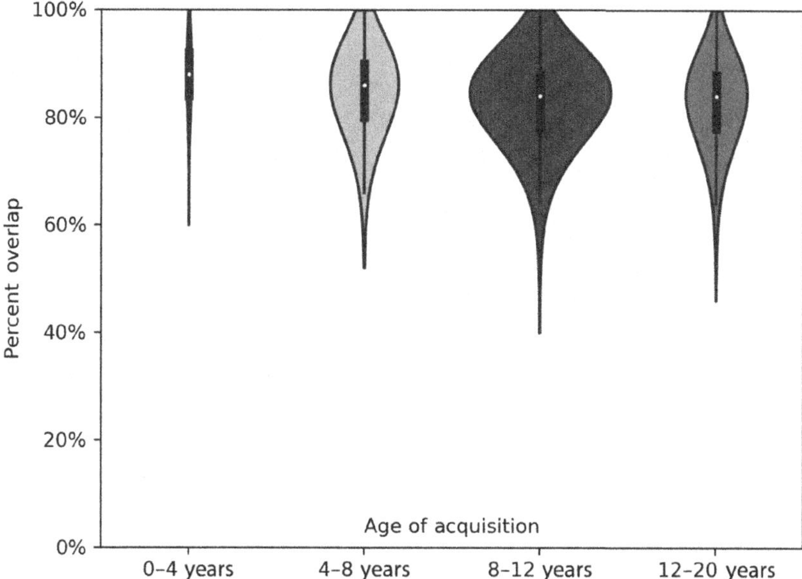

Figure 5 Nearest neighbor overlap for CBOW embeddings ($k = 50$). Higher overlap means that embeddings are more stable across random starts.

bin corresponds to the number of words in that bin, so that the 0–4 year group represents a smaller portion of the lexicon than the 8–12 year group. Thus, this figure shows that there is a high stability within these local embeddings, with an average of 84 percent. The CBOW embeddings are trained for 20 epochs with 100 negative samples per classification and subword n-grams ranging from 3 to 6.

Stability for the long-distance co-occurrence relationships captured by the SG embeddings is shown in Figure 6. We are again measuring the overlap between nearest neighbors for models trained on the different shuffles of the same corpus. The overall overlap here is lower, an average of 68 percent. This lower overlap results from the nature of the task: Here the model is optimized to predict the context given the target word and a wider range of factors influence this type of distribution. This remains, however, a relatively stable representation. The SG embeddings are trained for 20 epochs with 100 negative samples per classification and subword n-grams ranging from 3 to 6.

We have been using the local context captured by the CBOW task to represent syntactic information and the non-local context captured by the SG task to capture semantic information. However, there is no strict division between those factors which contribute to these two ways of viewing the distribution of words. How realistic is the assumption that these are two separate types of

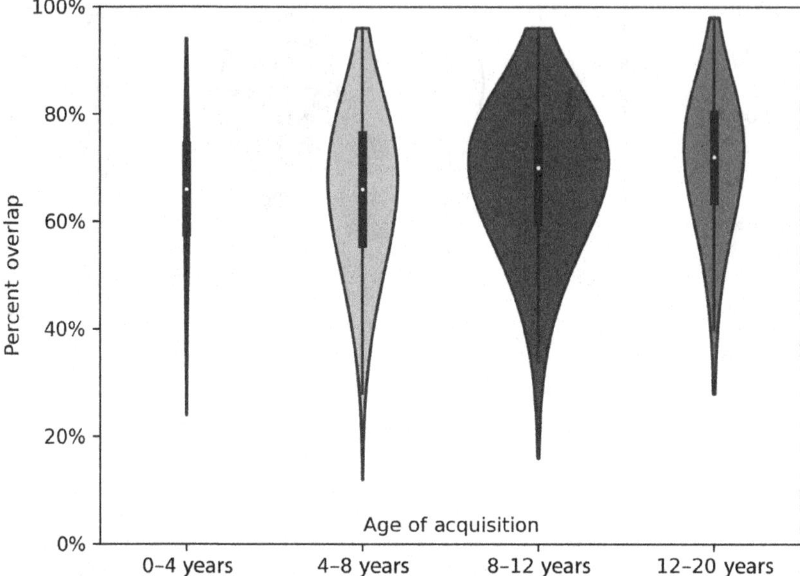

Figure 6 Nearest neighbor overlap for SG embeddings (k = 50). Higher overlap means that embeddings are more stable across random starts.

representation? In Figure 7 we compare the overlap of nearest neighbors across sets of embeddings in order to determine the degree to which these embeddings actually capture different aspects of co-occurrence. The basic question here is whether the local and non-local algorithms do, in fact, capture different linguistic attributes of word distribution. They do: The overall overlap is much lower than the stability measure above, with an average overlap of 21 percent. To summarize, then, this first set of evaluations tell us that each set of embeddings is relatively stable, although the local CBOW embeddings are more stable than the SG embeddings. And it also tells us that there is a minimum of information shared between the two optimization tasks. Thus, these embeddings represent two distinct types of linguistic behavior.

Although the embeddings are both stable and distinct, to what degree do they capture syntactic or semantic information? We can answer this for English using existing manual annotations. For each word in the lexicon, we take syntactic annotations from a participant-based concreteness task (Brysbaert, Warriner, & Kuperman, 2014) and semantic annotations from domains in the UCREL semantic tagger (Piao et al., 2015). These syntactic and semantic categorizations are not a part of the computational CxG itself. Rather, we are using them to understand the degree to which data-driven representations relate to introspective categorizations. An evaluation of the CBOW embeddings against

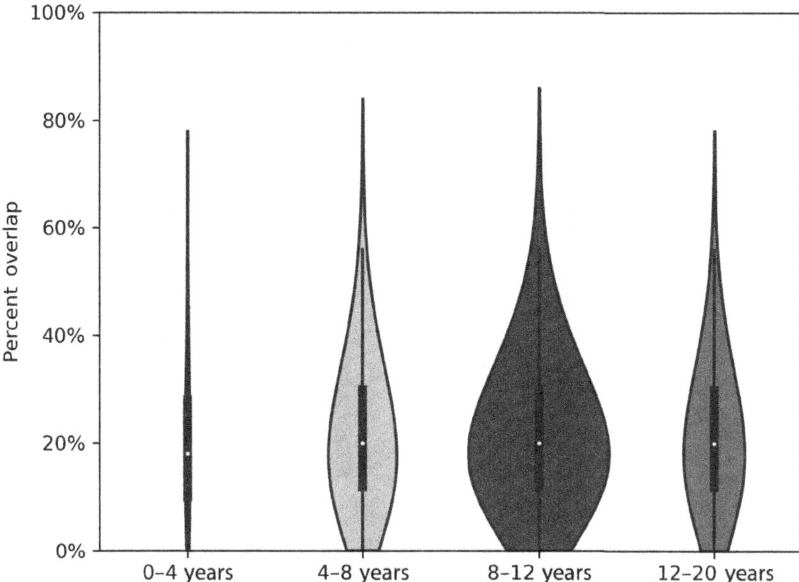

Figure 7 Nearest neighbor overlap for SG versus. CBOW embeddings (k = 50). Lower overlap means that the two sets of embeddings do not contain redundant or duplicated information.

syntactic annotations is shown in Figure 8 for eight parts of speech. For each word in the lexicon, we retrieve its five nearest neighbors using cosine distance. We then measure the overlap in annotations for each neighbor. For example, if a verb is most similar to four verbs and one noun, its overlap would be 4 out of 5 or 80 per cent. This measure of overlap captures the relationship between nearest neighbors in the embedding space and the discrete part-of-speech annotations. The bars measure the overlap of the model and provide a random baseline; given the large number of open-class nouns, for example, the random chance for overlap is rather high. While there is in no case a perfect alignment between introspection-based annotations and the nearest neighbors in the embeddings, there is a very significant overlap. The same measure of overlap is shown in Figure 9 between the SG embeddings and the semantic annotations, where each letter represents a specific high-level domain. The overlap here is lower on average, but as shown by the random baseline the correspondence remains highly significant: There is much more agreement between the embeddings and the annotations than by chance. Thus, we are using two sets of embeddings that capture different aspects of co-occurrence, each of which is relatively stable and largely overlaps with manual introspection-driven annotations.

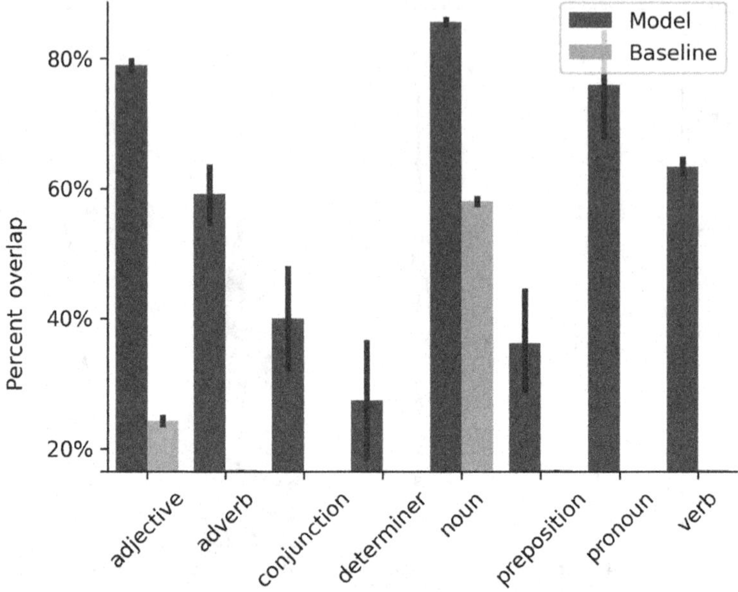

Figure 8 Percent nearest neighbors belonging to the same syntactic category. Higher values indicate that the CBOW embeddings capture syntactic information.

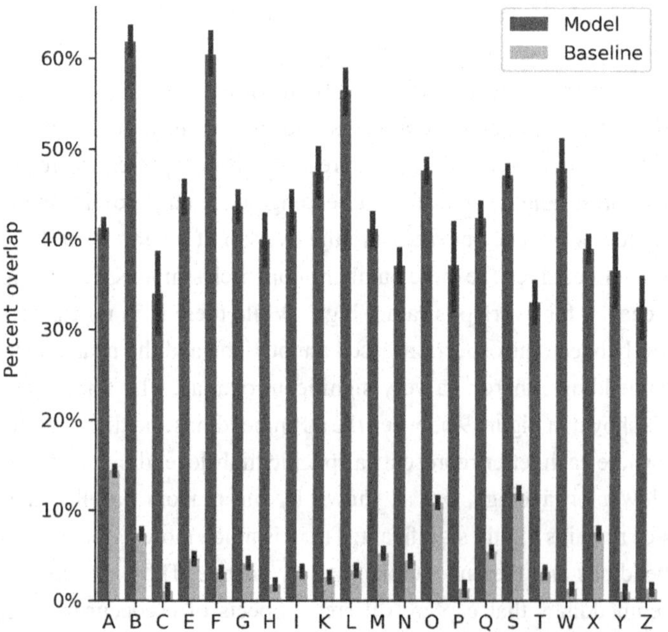

Figure 9 Percent nearest neighbors belonging to the same semantic category. Higher values indicate that the SG embeddings capture semantic information.

This discussion defends the decision to use a CBOW model for schematic syntactic information and a SG model for information about semantic frames. But why would we rely on non-contextual embeddings rather than context-specific transformer-based embeddings, such as those from BERT (Devlin et al., 2019)? First, we have a goal of understanding the degree to which grammatical structure, as described by CxG, can be learned from a reasonable amount of exposure. Because transformer-based models are trained on massive corpora, often exceeding 100 billion words, there is simply no way to understand the relationship between exposure and emergence given such methods. Second, the current state of our knowledge of word embeddings derived from the CBOW and SG tasks is much greater as these models are generally more transparent. The general approach to CxG described here is forwards-compatible with transformer-based language models; however, we formulate constraints in terms of non-contextual embeddings for these two reasons: the use of smaller corpora and the transparency of the algorithm. The main idea is the same: a distributed representation which is self-supervised in the sense that it is trained to predict the observed distribution of words in the background corpus. From this perspective, there is a family similarity between these embeddings and those which depend on the masked language modeling task (like BERT): The language learner is trying to understand what words will come next and every utterance in a corpus provides both positive and negative evidence that is used to support learning.

The traditional approach within linguistics is to rely on discrete categories like NOUN or VERB as slot-constraints, largely out of convenience. At the same time, we also expect from research in psycholinguistics that such categories have a prototype structure that is not captured by such discrete labels. The approach to slot-constraints taken here instead uses distributed representations (as would any transformer-based model). What is involved when we switch from a discrete to a distributed approach to representation? First, there is a robust line of work in computational linguistics showing that distributed representations provide better models of language than discrete representations (Bengio et al., 2003); this computational work is not incompatible with experimental linguistics. Second, there is a close correspondence between distributed word embeddings and association measures; for example, there is a close correspondence between a matrix of positive pointwise mutual information scores (a more traditional association measure) and SG embeddings with negative sampling (Levy et al., 2015). Essentially, this means that the network information contained in word embeddings is comparable to that contained in traditional association measures. But, fourth, the true strength of distributed word embeddings is not in the word vectors themselves in isolation but in the neighborhood similarity within the embedding space (cf., Linzen 2016). As explored in the next section, distributed representations are meaningful only within the context of a larger embedding space. Finally, fifth, when comparing distributed representations with discrete categories a common critique is that the distributed representations are *black boxes* of whose inner workings we have no understanding. On the contrary, we have a strong understanding of the behavior of these embedding spaces in terms of stability (Hellrich et al., 2019), in terms of cross-linguistic consistency (Burdick et al., 2021), in terms of cross-register consistency (Dunn, Li, & Sastre, 2022), and in terms of variation across dialects (Dunn, 2023b). While traditional linguistics is more comfortable with discrete representations, then, distributed representations are not black boxes.

1.4 Prototypes and Exemplars

In the previous section we used the CBOW and SG algorithms to learn word vectors to capture syntactic and semantic relationships between words, where *syntactic* relationships capture local adjacency and *semantic* relationships capture non-local co-occurrence patterns. Constructions consist of slot-constraints that define the set of words which can occupy a particular slot. In order to define a slot-constraint, we need to move from pairwise similarity relationships between words to groups of closely related words. In computational terms, this is a clustering problem that represents the formation of categories.

From the perspective of cognitive linguistics, we have two requirements for such a clustering algorithm: First, the clusters must have a prototype structure in which we can measure the degree to which a particular member is a central example of the category or a peripheral member. In computational terms, this means that we need to be able to determine how close to the centroid any particular example is. Second, the clusters must be centered around an exemplar which provides a good example for that category. Given these requirements, we use the K-MEDOIDS algorithm for clustering word embeddings into syntactic and semantic word classes (Schubert & Lenssen 2022; more precisely, the algorithm is called PAM for Partitioning Around Medoids).

$$cosine_{distance}(A,B) = 1 - \frac{A \cdot B}{\sqrt{A^2} * \sqrt{B^2}} \quad (4)$$

The k-medoids algorithm is a partioning approach to clustering, similar to k-means. The overall objective is to reform clusters until the all words are closest to their cluster center; while k-means quantifies the centroid of all words in a cluster using Euclidean distance, k-medoids uses an actual word as the centroid and allows other distance metrics. Here we use cosine distance, shown in equation (4). We previously used cosine similarity to define nearest neighbors within an embeddings space; cosine distance is the inverse of cosine similarity. The measure is the the dot product of two vectors (cf., equation [2]) normalized by the absolute values of those vectors, as shown in Equation (4). Thus, our category formation algorithm incorporates the previous definition of nearest neighbors within the embedding space.

We undertake clustering using the embedding spaces learned on the entire corpus collection to avoid the computational overhead of retraining these embeddings. However, the clustering itself only observes the specific lexicon found in a smaller set of exposure. For example, for this evaluation we observe 10 million words from the Project Gutenberg corpus, finding those lexical items which have a frequency of at least one part per million. With cosine distance for forming a network of relationships between words, the clusters are formed using only this subset of the vocabulary. K-medoids has access to the relationship between each word and every other word. Thus, larger vocabularies (the result of more exposure) have richer networks which, in turn, result in more precise syntactic and semantic categories. The evaluation here involves a lexicon of approximately 30k words.

Like k-means, the k-medoids algorithm requires a strict definition of *k*, the number of output clusters. The syntactic (CBOW) clusters need a smaller number of categories in order to provide a greater amount of generalization within each category. But the semantic (SG) clusters should allow a larger and more open-ended range of categories because the number of semantic domains is itself not particularly limited. Our basic approach is to define the range of numbers of categories for each type of constraint and then search for the exact number of categories which best describes the current lexicon. For syntactic categories, this search ranges from 25 to 250 and for semantic categories from 250 to 2,500. This search provides flexibility in finding the number of categories which best reflects the observed usage while still constraining the magnitude of the search space.

How do we know when the overall categorization with, say, 1,800 semantic domains is the best organization of the lexical network? We measure the quality of a clustering using the SILHOUETTE metric (Rousseeuw, 1987), which determines for each point how closely it fits into its current cluster and how distant it is from the surrounding clusters. The values range from -1 (a bad clustering) to 1 (a good clustering). For example, if we have too few semantic domains then the distance between words and their exemplar will generally be large. But if we have too many semantic domains there will be only a small distance between members of one category and the centroid of another. Both scenarios will reduce the silhouette metric, albeit for different reasons. Thus, while we define the magnitude of the number of clusters (in which we want fewer syntactic than semantic categories), the grammar itself is searching across specific clusterings.

Given that each cluster is defined by the exemplar that serves as its centroid, we name the clusters using several central examples to provide increased transparency in the constructional representations that we end up with. We also use cosine similarity to arrange the members of a cluster from central (a small distance from the exemplar) to peripheral (a large distance from the exemplar). From a usage-based perspective, the most frequent words will have unique behaviors. Thus, because category formation is about determining which words should be grouped together, we allow the most frequent words to occupy their own unique clusters. Here a *frequent* word accounts for at least 1 percent of the tokens in the learning corpus; in the 10 million word evaluation, that means a word must have 100k tokens to be given its own cluster. In the Project Gutenberg corpus, this includes: *it*, *i*, *he*, *was*, *that*, *in*, *a*, *to*, *and*, *of*, and *the*. In the semantic categories, these unique words remain unclustered because they are expected to occur equally across all semantic domains.

To summarize, we use k-medoids together with cosine distance to form syntactic and semantic categories which are centered around a specific exemplar and for which each individual member is quantified using its distance from that exemplar. We control the magnitude of the number of categories for each type of representation, but search for the best clustering using the silhouette measure. The most frequent words, hypothesized to have their own unique distribution, are assigned to their own clusters.

We have already seen that, when focusing on the nearest neighbors for each lexical item, each set of embeddings is relatively stable while still capturing different types of distributional relationships. And we have also seen that there is a significant correspondence between these distributional representations and discrete introspective annotations. The question now is, what kind of information do these larger categories capture after the clustering has taken place? Starting with the syntactic categories learned from the Project Gutenberg corpus, we see example clusters in Table 3, defined by their exemplar and then divided into central examples and peripheral examples.

These clusters are chosen in sequence, and show that each category is centered around a specific part of speech: nouns in #47, verbs in #46, adverbs in #44, and gerunds in #43. This explains the generally high agreement between nearest neighbors and manual annotations that we saw previously. Rather than high-level abstract syntactic categories, however, these categories reflect specific meanings and usages. For example, the nouns in #47 are all things that are pleasant to eat and the adverbs in #44 are centrally discourse markers. These

Table 3 Examples of syntactic categories from clustering CBOW embeddings.

#1 MOLASSES	#2: DISDAINED	#3: GENERALLY	#4: COMBINING
	Central examples		
scones	confounded	presumably	converting
cherries	exasperated	incidentally	framing
pickles	constrained	ostensibly	composing
spices	detested	consequently	modelling
dumplings	admonished	legitimately	mastering
	Peripheral examples		
ice	speaks	timely	organising
fungi	heed	publicly	landing
tea	obliged	extremely	including
drugs	exclaims	gladly	following
zinc	voted	absolutely	varying

Table 4 Examples of semantic categories from clustering SG embeddings.

#1: EXPLORATIONS	#2: ASSISTANT	#3: INTOLERABLE	#4: DANCING
	Central examples		
explorers	administrator	unendurable	dance
expeditions	manager	insupportable	romping
researches	associate	unbearable	waltzing
discoveries	superintendent	endure	masquerade
excursion	director	irksome	flirting

thus reflect subcategories from the perspective of a phrase structure grammar, categorizations which join form and usage together.

A selection of examples from the semantic categories is shown in Table 4, this time with only central examples because the larger number of categories much reduces the number of peripheral examples. Here we see how the skip-gram task focuses on semantic domains: In #1, for example, we see items from different syntactic categories that are a part of a single frame. In the same way, the examples in #3 are mostly adjectives but a verb (*endure*) is included as part of the same domain or frame. In this way, the semantic categories provide a larger number of related domains by which to define slots in constructions.

Table 5 Examples of syntagmatic (CBOW) versus Paradigmatic (SG) patterns (WK).

Syntagmatic	Paradigmatic	Syntagmatic	Paradigmatic
to flow		*criticism*	
builds	flows	complaint	criticisms
merge	flowing	annoyance	critique
extract	overflow	skepticism	critiques
search	overflowing	confirmation	critics
feed	meander	argument	constructive

When we manually inspect the syntactic and semantic categories, there is a clear meaning behind each cluster. But, given the possibility of instability in the embeddings themselves, how arbitrary are these clusters? To measure this, we undertake category formation on the same lexicon (from Project Gutenberg) using two distinct sets of embeddings, trained from different shufflings of the same corpus. We saw in Section 1.3 that these models are subject to a certain amount of instability. Does this instability mean that the categories that result from clustering are not reproducible? We measure the overlap between two sets of clusterings using the Adjusted Mutual Information score, which ranges from 0 (random clusterings) to 1 (complete agreement). In this setup, we observe a significant agreement of 0.66 (for syntactic categories from CBOW embeddings) and 0.58 (for semantic categories from SG embeddings). Thus, while there remains a certain amount of instability in the grammar, overall there is a significant relationship between independent clusterings.

A final way of contrasting these local versus non-local slot-constraints is to view the syntactic constraints as capturing syntagmatic relationships and the semantic constraints as capturing paradigmatic relationships. Two examples are given in Table 5, the verb "to flow" and the noun "criticism." In the first case, the syntactic category includes other verbs that would occupy the same position as "flow," while the semantic category includes other forms like "flowing" that are morphologically related. In the same way, the syntactic category with "criticism" includes other nouns which could be used in the same position, while the semantic category also includes different grammatical forms of the same lemma, like "criticisms" or "critics." While the categories cannot be defined perfectly as syntagmatic versus paradigmatic, this distinction is nonetheless useful for analyzing them.

The previous section presented and evaluated two types of word embeddings trained to represent syntactic and semantic relationships given the distributional patterns observed in a corpus. For the purposes of defining slots and slot-constraints, we must transform this network of pairwise relationships into categories. This section has presented an approach to category formation which centers each category around an exemplar and then arranges members of the category given their distance from that exemplar. These categories contain meaningful linguistic information and, while not perfectly stable, do show a significant relationship between independent clusterings.

1.5 Attraction: From Categories to Constraints

The grammar has so far focused on a usage-based approach to category formation, developing the basic ontology of representations required to capture lexical, syntactic, and semantic constraints. These are the basic constructions in the grammar. In this section we turn to the problem of ATTRACTION: How does a slot within a construction use these categories to attract certain slot-fillers?

First, how do we deal with OUT-OF-VOCABULARY words (henceforth, OOV) which are not contained in the lexicon and thus were not used during category formation? For example, the cluster evaluation in Section 1.4 worked with 10 million words from the Project Gutenberg corpus, with a frequency threshold of one part per million. This led to a lexicon containing approximately 30k word-forms. By OOV we mean those word-forms which were not assigned to clusters and thus will not be directly accessible for the purpose of forming or filling slot-constraints. In the first case our approach is to use the embedding for an unseen word to assign that OOV word to the nearest medoid (defined using cosine similarity).

While previous work has relied on discrete and uniform slot-constraints, we define constraints using distance from exemplars: Some members of a category are better examples and thus are better fillers for a slot. We exemplify this idea of prototype attractions in slot-constraints using the category memberships

Table 6 Members of semantic (left) and syntactic (right) domains.

SEM: DESCRIBES		SYN: SUPPOSE		SYN: EMBELLISHMENTS	
0.98	describing	0.92	pretend	0.94	adornments
0.98	illustrates	0.89	think	0.93	blandishments
0.98	relates	0.89	misunderstand	0.93	trappings
0.98	refers	0.88	believe	0.88	carvings
0.97	writes	0.88	expect	0.87	satire

shown in Table 6, with a semantic cluster on the left (#684) and two syntactic clusters on the right (#11 and #8). The central exemplar is shown in the header, while members of the cluster are listed together with their cosine similarity to the center (with higher values reflecting a better example). Because there are many more semantic clusters, each cluster is much smaller, which means that there are fewer distant members. With syntactic categories, however, there is a range of members further from the prototype.

(7) [SEM:684 – LEX:*what* – SYN:*HE* – SYN:11 – SYN:*IS* – SYN:*A/AN* – SYN:8]

(8) "He describes what he pretends is an embellishment."

(9) "He writes what he believes is a satire."

The potential construction in (7) follows our previous notational conventions but using constraints defined in reference to clusters. Recall that very frequent words are assigned to their own clusters, as we see here with, for example, *he*. The notation refers to individual clusters (i.e., SEM:#684), but computationally this is defined using the centroid or exemplar of that cluster: the word embedding which represents the prototype of that category. Thus, the utterance in (8) is a slightly better example of that potential construction in the sense that its slot-fillers are closer to the constraint's centroid. This idea allows us to use OOV words as fillers of slot-constraints using their distance to the exemplar rather than their discrete membership in the category.

A further problem is dealing with OOV words for which there is no embedding in the first place.[7] One advantage of the fastText character-based embeddings is that they are based on subword n-grams. Thus, the embeddings for a completely OOV word *judgements* could be easily reconstructed given the subword components of in-vocabulary words like *judge* and *judged* and *judgement*. Given this reconstructed embedding, this word would then be able to satisfy slot-constraints in the grammar.

We would expect that categories change as they are exposed to more usage: As the lexicon grows, the network of relationships between individual words grows denser and thus the categories become more precise. To model this, we investigate syntactic (local) categories from the Project Gutenberg corpus, with exposure ranging from 100k words to 10 million words. This is shown in Table 7 using the verbal category whose exemplar is *determined*. The top examples, all verbs at each level of exposure, express a meaning of the attitude of an individual toward some event. An outlier verb, *prepared*, which is less

[7] Because we trained the embeddings on a reference corpus of 2 billion words, many words which are not in the lexicon will still have embeddings in the model.

Table 7 Changes in category formation given increased exposure.

Exposure		#1	#2	#3	#4
100k	*Top*	determined	prepared	desired	compelled
	Bottom	*possible*	*anxious*	order	resolve
500k	*Top*	determined	permitted	prepared	compelled
	Bottom	*unable*	proceeds	begun	*vigilant*
1 mil	*Top*	determined	permitted	compelled	prepared
	Bottom	*willingness*	*impossible*	intend	*refusal*
2 mil	*Top*	determined	permitted	compelled	prepared
	Bottom	begun	*apt*	oblige	urge
5 mil	*Top*	determined	permitted	compelled	allowed
	Bottom	*apt*	hesitate	oblige	decide
10 mil	*Top*	determined	permitted	compelled	endeavoured
	Bottom	oblige	began	decide	begin

directly focused on attitude, slips out of the top set of examples as the network grows more robust with increased exposure. The bottom examples are those on the periphery, furthest from the exemplar. Here there are several non-verb examples (marked in italics). The number of non-verbs decreases as exposure increases, however, with only verbs remaining once we reach 10 million words of exposure. These examples show the way in which categories become more precise with increased exposure, with the observed changes taking place mostly in the periphery of the category.

1.6 Hierarchy: Relationships between Slots

We have so far put forward a replicable model of category formation, based on distribution, for the purpose of defining slot-constraints (basic constructions). A first-order construction is a sequence of slot-constraints that is defined by both the type of constraint (LEX, SYN, SEM) and the filler (which has a greater or lesser attraction to that slot). But is there structure within a first-order construction?

We begin the representation of structure within constructions using a measure of association. We previously used the normalized PMI to find lexical constructions (phrases); the advantage of the PMI family of association measures is that they provide a single value to measure the attraction between two words. In this case, however, we need to distinguish between the directions of

Table 8 Variables for calculating the ΔP.

	OUTCOME	NO OUTCOME	*Totals*
CUE	a	b	a + b
NO CUE	c	d	c + d
Totals	a + c	b + d	

association (left-to-right and right-to-left). We do this using the ΔP measure, developed with a focus on language learning (Ellis, 2007) and previously used for modelling the distribution of multi-word units in large corpora (Dunn, 2018c). The ΔP is particularly useful here because it allows for asymmetric associations: The issue of relationships between slots in a construction is not so much association strength on its own but rather the skew between the two direction-specific associations.

The basic idea behind the ΔP is to view a given word as a CUE and an adjacent word as an OUTCOME. For example, in the phrase "of course," the left-to-right association would view "of" as the cue and "course" as the outcome. As shown in Table 8, the measure is calculated by first counting the frequency of each cue with and without an outcome. Thus, the frequency of "of course" is *a* (cue and outcome together). The frequency of "of" on its own is *b* (the cue without the outcome). The frequency of "course" on its own is *c* (the outcome without the cue). And, finally, the variable *d* accounts for the general corpus size (the words which are neither cue nor outcome). The frequencies represented in the table thus can be used to measure the conditioning of particular outcomes given particular cues, originally situated within contingency learning (Ellis, 2007).

$$\Delta P = P(Outcome|Cue) - P(Outcome|NoCue) \tag{5}$$

The ΔP is the conditional probability of the outcome given the cue adjusted by the conditional probability of the outcome without the cue, as shown in equation (5). This is a directional or asymmetric measure of association because the role of cue and outcome can be calculated in either direction, as shown in Equations (6) and (7). In the left-to-right variant (ΔP_{LR}), the cue is the first word and the outcome is the second word, quantified as shown in equation (6). In the right-to-left variant (ΔP_{RL}), the cue is the second word and the outcome is the first word. Taken together, these measures connect corpus frequencies with contingency learning and provide direction-specific measures of association.

Table 9 Examples of directional differences in association.

Equal directions	LR dominant	RL dominant
[terror – stricken]	[on > horseback]	[connected < with]
[royal – academy]	[had > elapsed]	[kissed < her]
[standing – upright]	[his > patron]	[obliged < to]
[sudden – flood]	[it > happens]	[committee < on]
[northern – hemisphere]	[a > dozen]	[examine < it]
[wild – beasts]	[have > climbed]	[willing < to]
[six – ounces]	[from > northwest]	[series < of]
[second – mate]	[by > jove]	[buried < in]
[full – swing]	[which > stretches]	[belongs < to]
[get – rid]	[an > eternity]	[refer < to]

$$\Delta P_{LR} = \frac{a}{a+c} - \frac{b}{b+d} \tag{6}$$

$$\Delta P_{RL} = \frac{a}{a+b} - \frac{c}{c+d} \tag{7}$$

We include this association-based information about structure in the notation used for constructions. If the association between two adjacent slot-constraints is symmetric (i.e., there is no significant difference between the direction-specific measures), we use the previous notation "–". But if the association is asymmetric we use "<" to indicate that the right-to-left variant is stronger and ">" to indicate that the left-to-right variant is stronger. This captures local dominance in the relationships between adjacent slot-constraints.

The difference in direction of association is shown in Table 9 from 100k words of the Project Gutenberg corpus. The table shows pairs of slot-constraints with equal association in each direction, with a dominant left-to-right association, and with a dominant right-to-left association. In the first case, pairs with equal association in each direction are phrases such as *terror stricken* or *standing upright* in which both words have an equal standing. With a dominant left-to-right association, however, we instead see pairs like *on horseback* or *a dozen* in which the first word is quite common and thus occurs with many other pairs while the second word is fairly restricted to this particular phrase. Similarly, with a dominant right-to-left association we see pairs like *obliged to* and *belongs to* in which the second word occurs after a large number of other items but the first word is restricted to this particular combination.

While introspective linguistic analysis has focused on discrete relationships between slots (such as case roles like AGENT or DIRECT OBJECT), this approach uses continuous distributional relationships instead. This notion of hierarchy provides an analysis of structure within the construction. Here we show only the association between lexical constraints, but of course the grammar itself has access to both syntactic and semantic constraints as well and dominance is indicated between each pair of constraints in a construction. While we have conceptualized a construction as a sequence of slot-constraints, we could as easily have drawn from dependency grammar and conceptualized a construction as dependency relationships between slot-constraints, as hinted at here using association. The expansion of computational CxG from sequence-based to dependency-based representations remains a challenge for future work.

1.7 Computational versus Cognitive Representations

In Section 1 we have focused on a usage-based computational representation of constructions: the data-driven emergence of atomic slot-constraints (basic constructions). We began with the lexicon itself, the core inventory of word-forms available to the learner, using a measure of association (the NPMI) to find lexical constructions. We then focused on categories of words, using distributional information in the form of word embeddings (both the CONTINUOUS-BAG-OF-WORDS and the SKIP-GRAM variants). These embeddings situated the vocabulary in a vector space, a network of relationships which we used to build clusters and to provide central exemplars for each cluster. Finally, we used association measures (the ΔP) to consider relationships between slots within a construction. Thus, our primitive representations are word-forms, categories of words, and relations between contiguous slots in a construction. What is the relationship between these computational representations and the representations of actual learners?

The first fundamental difference between computational and cognitive representations is the MEANS OF EXPOSURE. For a human language learner, the input consists of (i) the usage or production of others, (ii) observations of the external physical and social context, and (iii) potentially a genetic predisposition of some sort toward language. For a computational model of language learning, however, the input consists of (i) the usage or production contained in a corpus and (ii) the assumptions of the computational framework. For instance, previous work in computational CxG assumed the universal part-of-speech tagset, so that a learner would begin with a distinction between nouns and verbs (Dunn, 2022a). Because it is notoriously difficult to untangle the influence of both the stimuli and the language faculty in human language learning, our ability to experiment with different starting assumptions in a computational framework provides an important way to test the degree to which language is learnable from exposure alone. In other words, if a computational model can adequately learn a grammar from input, it follows that a human learner *could* do the same as well. The challenge, though, is that the external physical and social experience of a human learner is missing from a computational framework. Thus, in cases where a computational model is inadequate, is it due to missing these experiences or is it due to missing the genetic predispositions of the language faculty?

The second fundamental difference is that computational representations (of all varieties) are ultimately ISOMORPHIC rather than substantive in their semantics. This isomorphism means that our representations should enter into all of the same relationships as would a speaker's cognitive representations. For example, if speakers judge *flower* and *plant* to be more similar than *flower* and *house*, our computational representations should mirror this similarity. Thus, our syntactic and semantic representations provide a network of pairwise relationships between words. This is also true for knowledge-based approaches, which usually depend on an ontology that manually specifies such relationships, albeit in a discrete form (Nirenburg & Raskin, 2004). Beyond this network of relationships, however, there is no substance behind computational representations that would be similar to the idea of embodied experience that some cognitive linguists have offered as a foundation for semantics (Lakoff & Johnson, 1999). While the semantics of cognitive representations might be embedded in physical experience, the semantics of any computational representations is purely a matter of isomorphic relationships.

A third difference, perhaps less fundamental, has to do with the type of usage that is observed. For the computational experiments here, we draw from a number of registers, as shown in Table 1. These are ultimately all written registers, with differences in the situational parameters that we could use to describe their context of production (Biber & Conrad, 2009). These different situational parameters, in turn, lead to somewhat different structural patterns. The issue is that human learners are first exposed to spoken rather than written usage. Although we can control for the amount of exposure (cf., Section 3.2), we have less control over the register of exposure.

These are the three main distinctions between computational and cognitive representations within CxG: the means of exposure, the source of semantics, and the register of exposure. These are the primary ways in which a corpus-based computational experiment differs from an experiment conducted on human participants. Given these differences, why should we rely on computational experiments at all? There are three primary advantages of a computational approach to CxG: First, the scope of computational experiments can mimic actual language learning in a way that laboratory experiments cannot, in terms of (i) the number of participants observed, (ii) the number of grammatical structures observed, and (iii) the number of languages and dialects observed. Second, the exposure conditions of computational experiments can precisely define how much and what sorts of input the learner has experienced in a way that laboratory experiments could never practically achieve. Third, the role of the language faculty (as opposed to exposure) is easier to demarcate in a computational framework, as is the relationship between additional assumptions and increased grammar quality.

A discovery-device grammar, which combines mechanisms of emergence with the precise evaluation of grammar quality, has been viewed as the highest form of linguistic theory (Goldsmith, 2015). Inspired by work in machine learning, we conceptualize such a model of grammar as (i) a defined hypothesis space of potential constructions, (ii) a search method or discovery procedure for navigating these potential representations, and (iii) a loss function or evaluation metric for guiding the search toward better representations. Much like the linguistic experience of individual language learners, a corpus is always a somewhat arbitrary collection of utterances. The question is, how do we ensure robust generalizations when we observe only a limited sample of usage?

In computational terms, we use three main approaches to ensure robust generalizations during the learning process. The first problem is that unobserved structures (OUT-OF-VOCABULARY) are difficult to model. The solution here is to use character-based embeddings to estimate word vectors for such out-of-vocabulary items and then leverage the prototype structure of categories to allow for out-of-vocabulary slot-fillers (cf., in Section 1.5). The second problem is that different corpora represent specific domains and the generalizations based on those corpora decline in quality as we move further away from the original domain. This is a problem of *domain adaptation*; recent work has made it possible to measure such domain differences (Li & Dunn, 2022; Li, Dunn, & Nini, 2022) with a focus on dialect and register. Our basic approach to domain adaption here is to implement smoothing, which removes probability mass from observed items, thus leaving space for unobserved items (cf., Section 2.1). The third problem is that a learning algorithm is influenced by the order and the spacing of specific observations; for example, a model might be biased toward examples that were frequent early in its training period. We consider this in the form of a hypothesis about FORGETTING constructions, in which periods of learning are interspersed with periods of forgetting in order to establish more robust generalizations (cf., Section 3.1).

2 Learning Constructions

This second section presents a computational approach to learning constructions. We want to know which constructions are entrenched given the evidence of production from a particular corpus. The usage-based model of category formation from Section 1 provides an emerging ontology of slot-constraints (basic constructions). How do these constraints coalesce into first-order constructions? This problem requires measuring properties of each potential construction, such as its frequency and its association, in order to determine which potential constructions are in fact productive. From a computational perspective, this is a search problem and we must define the hypothesis space of potential constructions before developing a method for exploring this hypothesis space. From a usage-based perspective, this search problem models the mechanisms by which constructions emerge from observed usage, the second component of a discovery-device grammar.

How do we know when a particular pattern or chunk has become a construction? Here we have two related concepts: A CHUNK is a pattern or sequence from a corpus and a CONSTRUCTION is a grammatical description which represents the productive linguistic knowledge of a community of speaker-hearers. Both chunks and constructions would be represented using the ontology of slot-constraints developed in Section 1. And in both cases these structures are specific to a corpus drawn from a community rather than to a language as a whole. In other words, it only makes sense to talk about the entrechment of a chunk or construction relative to some population for which it is entrenched. The distinction between a chunk and a construction has to do with its status in the grammar: A chunk is a potential construction, while a construction proper is one which is contained in the constructicon. Thus, the term *chunk* provides a convenient way to refer to potential constructions which exist in the hypothesis space for the grammar but not necessarily in the grammar itself.

An overview of this section is shown in Figure 10. We begin by exploring corpus-based measures of entrenchment that evaluate whether a chunk is a productive construction (Section 2.1). Given these measures, we approach the problem of searching across sequences of potential slot-constraints to provide an inventory of potential constructions (Section 2.2). We evaluate potential grammars using the Minimum Description Length paradigm, which requires both a measure of grammar complexity (Section 2.3) and a measure of the grammar's ability to describe a test corpus, both expressed as encoding size (Section 2.4). This evaluation metric reflects the need to balance memory and computation in usage-based grammar, finding the right mix

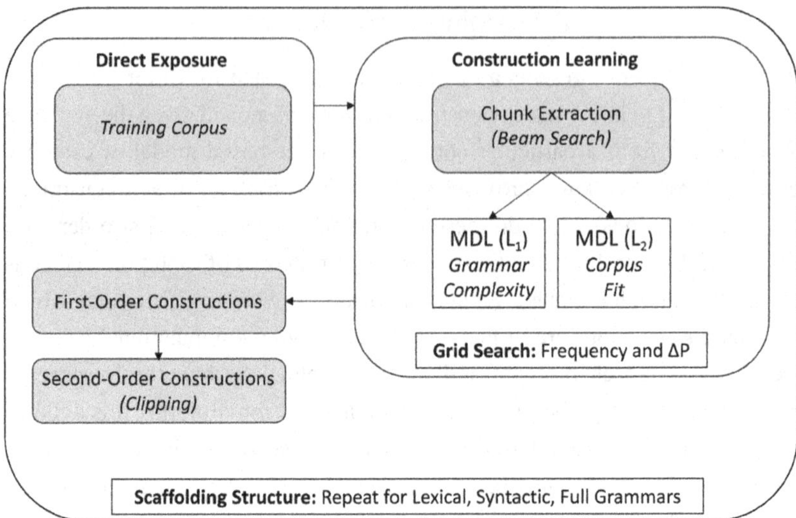

Figure 10 Learning a grammar of constructions (parsing and evaluating constructions)

between storing irregular forms and assembling predictable forms. This metric is then used to guide a grid-search across different frequency and association thresholds.

One of the ongoing challenges for usage-based syntax is the *projection problem*, in which the learner must first posit grammatical structure for an utterance in order for that utterance to then count as meaningful exposure. We consider this, as well as the general problem of parsing construction grammars, in Section 2.5. In Section 2.6 we introduce a distinction between first-order and second-order constructions in order to support a more precise description of the constructicon: A SECOND-ORDER CONSTRUCTION is one which has been formed indirectly by merging two existing constructions together. Finally, as emerging structures become more complex, we face the problem of levels of abstraction, with some chunks quite item specific and others quite generalized. We present an iterative approach to scaffolding structure during learning in Section 2.7, in which the same discovery-device construction grammar is used to acquire first lexical-only constructions, then syntactic-only constructions, and finally a full constructicon which incorporates all three types of slot-constraints. Thus, this section focuses on the mechanisms by which, given an emerging ontology of slot-constraints, the grammar itself emerges from observed usage.

2.1 Measuring Entrenchment: Frequency, Association, and Smoothing

A *chunk* or potential construction is a sequence of these learned slot-constraints which needs to be considered for possible inclusion in the grammar: Some chunks will become entrenched given continued usage but most will not. The set of chunks which must be considered for inclusion in the grammar makes up the hypothesis space for grammar learning.

To quantify this hypothesis space, we use 10 million words to find the number of pairwise sequences once we include syntactic and semantic slot-constraints: the news comments corpus (CM), the Twitter corpus (TW), the Wikipedia corpus (WK), the European Parliament corpus (EU), and the Project Gutenberg corpus (PG). This is shown in Table 10, where all sequences which occur at least twice are included. These frequencies show us the sheer size of the hypothesis space even when the size of a construction is constrained to just two slots: The totals range from 1.99 (EU) to 3.30 million (TW and WK).

The most common sequences contain lexical constraints, starting with the largest category (LEX – LEX). Following this, semantic sequences are more common than syntactic sequences. This order is caused by our category formation processes: There are approximately 30k words in the lexicon, 2.5k semantic categories, and 250 syntactic categories. More categories leads to both more sequence types and a lower per-type frequency. This is what we want in order to capture different levels of abstraction within constructions.

The problem, then, is to filter this set of chunks in order to find those which are more likely to be entrenched. In the first case, any particular chunk must be sufficiently frequent before it can be considered entrenched. This threshold-based approach only considers frequency as a cutting mechanism to remove certain items from consideration. The same frequency threshold is used as when forming the lexicon: one part per million. The impact of this threshold is shown in the bottom portion of Table 10.

The number of sequences is substantially lower, ranging now from 526k (EU) to 658k (TW). Thus, frequency alone can be used to reduce the hypothesis space. A large number of chunks remain, however. Thus, we also draw on an association measure, the direction-specific ΔP that was presented in Section 1.6. Our goal is not only to calculate association for a given corpus but also to generalize entrenchment across a particular population of speaker-hearers. This generalization problem is well explored within natural language processing in the form of probability smoothing. Highly frequent items or sequences tend to generalize well across corpora; the difficulty is working with rare or even unseen items

Table 10 Number of pairwise sequences by constraint type and corpus.

	NC	TW	WK	EU	PG
Before frequency threshold					
LEX – LEX	581,754	619,131	578,911	432,655	586,384
SEM – LEX	410,744	483,873	469,016	295,188	412,216
LEX – SEM	409,003	476,917	463,346	293,946	413,000
LEX – SYN	375,267	441,679	427,430	261,021	392,049
SYN – LEX	372,513	446,238	433,497	254,330	374,877
SEM – SEM	224,496	306,357	277,778	163,694	212,601
SEM – SYN	181,979	234,618	192,723	126,394	178,093
SYN – SEM	181,252	231,317	193,852	124,395	175,684
SYN – SYN	57,497	64,194	57,607	46,172	56,459
Total	**2,794,505**	**3,304,324**	**3,094,160**	**1,997,795**	**2,801,363**
After frequency threshold					
LEX – LEX	97,255	89,138	87,100	87,923	95,280
SEM – LEX	85,053	83,680	85,699	71,797	84,632
LEX – SEM	84,905	83,724	84,109	71,551	83,130
LEX – SYN	78,268	79,291	79,024	67,574	76,761
SYN – LEX	79,943	81,218	82,045	67,360	76,245
SEM – SEM	58,532	64,807	67,734	48,068	58,224
SEM – SYN	55,292	66,091	63,563	43,353	54,140
SYN – SEM	55,266	66,924	63,639	42,572	51,792
SYN – SYN	35,548	43,895	37,170	26,782	35,317
Total	**630,062**	**658,768**	**650,083**	**526,980**	**615,521**

that do not appear in the training corpus. Just because a particular sequence has not been observed does not mean that sequence is not possible.

The essential problem which smoothing is designed to address is the presence of out-of-vocabulary items whose frequencies cannot be captured using training corpora. While the embeddings used for category formation can be used to assign out-of-vocabulary words to existing word classes, sequences which are unattested in the training data remain difficult to generalize. One effective type of smoothing is *absolute discounting*, which reduces the frequencies of observed sequences in order to leave probability mass available for new unseen sequences. A further refinement, called Kneser-Ney discounting (Kneser & Ney, 1995), quantifies the continuation probability for each

Table 11 Variables for calculating the ΔP with smoothing.

	$freq(pair) = freq(pair) - \delta$	
	OUTCOME	**NO OUTCOME**
CUE	$a = freq(pair)$	$b = freq(item1) - a$
NO CUE	$c = freq(item2) - a$	$d = total - a - b - c$

sequence: This is the idea that some items occur in diverse contexts (like "of X"), while other items occur in a limited number of contexts (like "X course"). This type of discounting is not necessary with the ΔP because this measure already controls for the presence of the cue without the outcome.

Borrowing this idea from statistical language models, we add smoothing to the ΔP in order to increase its ability to generalize across corpora. We calculate the rate of discounting by dividing the training corpus into two parts, calculating the frequency of all pairwise sequences in the first part and then finding the difference between the first part and the second. We calculate a discounting rate for each of the nine sequence types shown in Table 10 (i.e., LEX-LEX). Following previous work, we also calculate a unique discounting rate for individual frequency strata (Chen & Goodman, 1999). Thus, the rate of smoothing is empirically fitted to both the type of sequence and its frequency, so that less frequent sequences can receive a higher degree of smoothing. Table 11 shows how the smoothing adjusts the frequencies used to calculate the ΔP. The frequency of the sequence in question is adjusted by the discount rate (cf., Table 12) and this then influences the other frequencies accordingly.

The range of discounting values is shown in Table 12 across sequence type and frequency strata for two corpora, Project Gutenberg and Wikipedia, each with two subsets of 5 million words each. The importance of calculating the discount rate separately for each type and frequency strata is shown by the range of values: Some have a very low discount rate (such as SEM – SYN at 0.18 and 0.12), which means that the difference in frequencies for this type of sequence across different corpora is itself quite small. This is not a surprising finding because these more general constraint types are less dependent on specific utterances. But more item-specific sequences (such as LEX – LEX) have a much higher discount rate, closer to 1. We have thus tailored the smoothing rate to the specific frequency patterns of each sequence type.

We evaluate the degree to which this smoothing influences the ΔP in Table 13, which shows the Pearson correlation between the smoothed and raw association for the Wikipedia corpus, divided by sequence type and frequency

Table 12 Discounting values, δ, by sequence type and frequency strata. This indicates the magnitude of frequency smoothing at different levels.

	PG				WK			
Type	**F=1**	**F=2**	**F=3**	**F>3**	**F=1**	**F=2**	**F=3**	**F>3**
LEX – LEX	0.64	0.73	0.78	0.83	0.66	0.78	0.83	0.94
LEX – SYN	0.47	0.63	0.71	0.74	0.47	0.66	0.73	0.88
LEX – SEM	0.56	0.64	0.68	0.72	0.57	0.72	0.76	0.87
SYN – SYN	0.42	0.25	0.16	0.08	0.50	0.29	0.21	0.32
SYN – LEX	0.48	0.64	0.70	0.71	0.46	0.64	0.71	0.88
SYN – SEM	0.20	0.37	0.47	0.53	0.12	0.27	0.36	0.66
SEM – SEM	0.52	0.60	0.58	0.50	0.44	0.60	0.61	0.76
SEM – SYN	0.18	0.34	0.41	0.54	0.12	0.29	0.34	0.66
SEM – LEX	0.57	0.63	0.68	0.72	0.57	0.70	0.76	0.88

Table 13 Correlation between smoothed and raw ΔP by sequence type and frequency strata (Wikipedia corpus). This indicates the overall impact of frequency smoothing on association values.

Freq.	**Type**	**N**	**r(ΔP_{LR})**	**r(ΔP_{RL})**
<5	LEX – SEM	148,255	0.34	0.98
5–10	LEX – SEM	62,656	0.56	0.99
10–100	LEX – SEM	71,915	0.57	0.99
100–200	LEX – SEM	5,076	0.70	0.99
>200	LEX – SEM	4,694	0.77	0.99
<5	SEM – LEX	149,306	0.97	0.47
5–10	SEM – LEX	64,754	0.99	0.64
10–100	SEM – LEX	73,712	1.00	0.74
100–200	SEM – LEX	5,011	0.99	0.87
>200	SEM – LEX	4,350	0.98	0.89
<5	SEM – SEM	82,664	0.36	0.40
5–10	SEM – SEM	38,173	0.55	0.61
10–100	SEM – SEM	53,878	0.52	0.62
100–200	SEM – SEM	6,108	0.46	0.74
>200	SEM – SEM	8,114	0.54	0.64

strata; to save space, only select semantic constraints are shown. All correlations are significant at the $p < 0.001$ level. We expect that more frequent sequences are less influenced by smoothing because the discount rate is small relative to the overall frequency. But less frequent sequences will be heavily influenced because the discount rate will constitute a large portion of their overall frequency.

In most cases, more frequent categories have a higher correlation between smoothed and raw association values. For example, in LEX – SEM sequences in the left-to-right direction, there is a small but significant correlation of 0.34 in the low frequency band that increases consistently to 0.77 in the highest frequency band. This means that the impact of smoothing is highest on those items which are observed only a few times. The impact of smoothing on semantic constraints is larger in general than on lexical constraints. This frequency-based effect of smoothing is precisely what we expect since highly frequent items will provide a better initial estimate of association than rare items.

This section has focused on reducing and exploring the hypothesis space of chunks – potential constructions that need to be considered while learning a grammar. We started with a measure of association, the ΔP, because sequences of slot-constraints which are not expected to follow one another are also not likely to be entrenched. The number of chunks remains high, however, so we use a frequency threshold to further limit the number of sequences. Lexical constraints are more influenced by a frequency threshold and syntactic constraints are less influenced. Finally, we introduced smoothing for the ΔP in order to increase our ability to generalize away from the training corpus. The basic idea behind our discount-based smoothing is that less frequent sequences will be subject to more arbitrary variation and thus should be subject to a higher degree of smoothing.

2.2 Searching for Chunks: Beyond Templates

Given a large hypothesis space of these chunks (cf., Table 10), we use a beam search parsing strategy to determine which of them have been sufficiently entrenched to be treated as constructions proper. An alternate approach to this problem, taken in previous work, is to base the search around fixed templates (Dunn, 2017; Perek & Patten, 2019), where the templates or patterns are defined by hand. There are three weaknesses with relying on manually defined templates: First, templates rely on fixed syntactic categories (like nouns and verbs), even though such basic categories should themselves be emerging structures. Second, the design of these templates is language specific and introduces assumed linguistic knowledge. Third, one of our goals is to determine

Table 14 Potential chunks for related utterances. This shows how very similar utterances could be used to learn different constructional representations.

	Slot 1	Slot 2	Slot 3	Slot 4
LEX	send	me	a	receipt
SYN	VERB	PRN	DET	NOUN
SEM	*<transfer>*	*<speaker>*	*<none>*	*<financial>*
LEX	email	me	a	copy
SYN	VERB	PRN	DET	NOUN
SEM	*<transfer>*	*<speaker>*	*<none>*	*<abstract>*
LEX	give	me	a	call
SYN	VERB	PRN	DET	NOUN
SEM	*<transfer>*	*<speaker>*	*<none>*	*<communicate>*
LEX	give	me	a	break
SYN	VERB	PRN	DET	NOUN
SEM	*<transfer>*	*<speaker>*	*<none>*	*<leisure>*

the influence of increased exposure on increasingly complex constructions, a phenomenon that would be disguised by relying on pre-defined templates. For these reasons we develop an approach that relies on a beam search across alternate pathways through slot-constraints (Dunn, 2019a).

The underlying assumption is that every utterance has been produced or licensed by an entrenched construction. That entrenched construction could range from an item-specific lexical phrase (the least abstract) to a fully syntactic phrase structure rule (the most abstract). The challenge is to find the chunk – the specific sequence of slot-constraints – which best captures the linguistic properties of that sequence across the corpus.

Consider the examples in Table 14, which are shown using lexical, syntactic, and semantic constraints (these are based on introspection simply for the sake of exposition and are not a result of computational CxG). The phenomenon of interest here is the difference between one type of slot-constraint and another. All four utterances could be described using a variant of the ditransitive construction in (10). However, the idiomatic final example *give me a break* could also be described using the item-specific construction in (11). The challenge for the chunking algorithm is to allow weak links within a construction without pre-defining a set of possible constructional shapes. In other words, we need to ensure that both the generalized construction in (10) and the item-specific construction in (11) are allowed to emerge.

Table 15 Beam search algorithm for chunk selection.

Variables

node = slot-constraint in the input corpus
startingNode = start of potential construction
state = type of slot-constraint for node
path = route from root to successor states
$[c]$ = list of immediate successor states
c_i, c_{i+1} = transition to successor constraint
candidateStack = plausible constructions
evaluate = maximize $\sum(\Delta P_{LR} + \Delta P_{RL})$ for c_i, c_{i+1} in *path*

Main loop

```
for each possible startingNode in line:
   RecursiveSearch(path = startingNode)
evaluate candidateStack
horizontal pruning (remove nested chunks)
frequency pruning (remove infrequent chunks)
```

Recursive function

```
RecursiveSearch(path):
   for c_i, c_{i+1} in [c] from path:
      if max(ΔP_LR, ΔP_RL) of c_i, c_{i+1} > threshold:
         add c_{i+1} to path
         RecursiveSearch(path)
      else if path is >= 2 and <= 9:
         add to candidateStack
```

(10) [*transfer* – PRN – DET – NOUN]

(11) [*transfer* – PRN – DET – "break"]

The beam search algorithm is defined in Table 15. The basic idea is to thread a highly associated path through the slot-constraints of potential constructions in order to find those which may be entrenched. These chunks are evaluated using directional pairwise association, so that the optimal next slot-constraint will be associated with the current slot-constraint. Such a measure has a local bias because its immediate memory is limited to the current transition or choice of next slot-constraint (not unlike a bigram language model).

Thus, the beam search allows many candidates to be found from the same starting position (i.e., slot) and then undertakes a global evaluation of competing candidates. The sequence with the highest association (including both the left-to-right and the right-to-left directions) is retained. This references the *total association* of a particular sequence, which is the accumulated sum of each pairwise association within the sequence.

The use of total association is a way to prefer longer constructions without explicitly coding such a preference: Longer constructions will have more slot-constraints and thus have more opportunity to accumulate association across pairs of constraints. Chunks must contain between two and nine slots chosen because of known memory constraints on sequence chunking (Miller, 1956). Low and negative association values indicate that a particular item is repelled from a position in the chunk; thus, while longer sequences may contain a slot with low association it is quite unlikely that they would contain a repelled slot with negative association.

For each sentence in the input, the global evaluation compares the set of candidates from each starting node, taking the one which maximizes total association. Because a highly associated sequence, with differing starting nodes, would lead to multiple partially aligned variants, a horizontal pruning algorithm is used to remove those chunks which are wholly contained within another chunk. A final pruning stage parses each of the candidates in the corpus and evaluates them against a frequency threshold. This leads to two parameters in the algorithm: the pairwise association threshold for continuing a particular line of search and a corpus-wide frequency threshold for discarding rare chunks.

The size of the hypothesis space extracted by this algorithm is shown in Table 16 for the news comments corpus (CM), the Wikipedia corpus (WK), and the Twitter corpus (TW) at a size of 1 million words. The final frequency threshold is fixed at five parts per million and the ΔP threshold ranges from 0.05 to 0.35. Higher values lead to fewer but more entrenched chunks. It is clear

Table 16 Size of candidate space by ΔP threshold and frequency threshold. The candidate space is the number of potential constructions observed.

	NC		WK		TW	
	ΔP	*Freq*	ΔP	*Freq*	ΔP	*Freq*
$\Delta P = 0.05$	42,879	9,439	47,022	12,265	30,811	7,086
$\Delta P = 0.10$	18,541	5,204	26,822	8,311	12,348	3,757
$\Delta P = 0.15$	10,446	3,361	14,861	5,530	5,791	2,213
$\Delta P = 0.20$	5,869	2,194	8,323	3,761	3,097	1,417
$\Delta P = 0.25$	3,569	1,508	3,585	2,176	1,750	932
$\Delta P = 0.30$	2,228	1,075	2,333	1,549	1,042	627
$\Delta P = 0.35$	1,494	803	1,733	1,213	705	474

that these two thresholds have a significant impact on the extraction algorithm, essentially tuning the relative size of the hypothesis space. The question, then, is how to determine those thresholds in a reasonable manner. To answer this question, we need a measure of how complex each potential grammar is and how well it describes a test corpus, the problems addressed in the next two sections. As shown in Figure 10, we use a grid search across thresholds (with ΔP values ranging from 0.05 to 0.40), choosing the exact threshold empirically against the training corpus. In order to do this, however, we first need to develop the Minimum Description Length metric for evaluating grammars.

2.3 Grammar Complexity: Storage versus Computation

Having found chunks in a corpus of usage, the next challenge is to determine which have become entrenched as constructions. We have also seen that the ΔP threshold and the frequency threshold chosen for the beam search algorithm have significant impacts on the size of the grammar. This means that we also need to avoid arbitrarily selecting a threshold, so that the downstream properties of the grammar depend on arbitrary choices in the model. For these reasons we use the Minimum Description Length paradigm (MDL: Grünwald, 2007) to provide a metric of grammar quality that balances the need for both memory (storing potentially redundant item-specific constructions) and computation (reassembling more abstract constructions as needed).

(12) [SYN: DET – SYN: ADJ – SYN: N]

(13) [SYN: DET – SYN: ADJ – SEM: *<idea>*]

(14) [SYN: DET – LEX: “broken” – LEX: “heart”]

From a usage-based perspective, any sequence in the corpus *could* be stored in the grammar, where the term GRAMMAR is ambiguous between a computational model and the linguistic competence of a community of speaker-hearers. Consider the constructions in (12) through (14) which vary in their level of abstractness. In (12) a phrase structure rule is created by relying on purely syntactic constraints. In (13) a semantic constraint restricts this to nouns from a particular semantic frame. And, finally, the lexical constraints in (14) create an item-specific construction, in essence a collocation. These constructions are redundant in the sense that a phrase like “a broken heart” would be described or licensed by all three constructions. Given the linguistic behavior observed in a corpus, however, we might well hypothesize that all three constructions are simultaneously entrenched in the grammar of the community being represented. On the one extreme, a grammar of only phrase structure rules would poorly describe the usage in the corpus by ignoring irregular and item-specific behaviors. On the other extreme, a grammar which stores each phrase would make poor generalizations and, failing to make generalizations, would provide a poor description of the corpus. The challenge here is to balance memory and computation in the grammar.

The basic idea in MDL is to quantify both (i) the complexity of the grammar and (ii) the fit between the grammar and a corpus. The complexity of the grammar is used to represent the cost of storage. The fit between the grammar and a test corpus is used to represent the computational gain of storage. Thus, storing an item-specific construction is worthwhile when that construction improves our ability to describe the corpus. An alternate way of viewing this problem of what makes a construction worth learning has to do with idiosyncracy: Any construction which is idiosyncratic or in some way unique in form or meaning must be stored (Goldberg, 2006). Thus, in (14) the phrase "broken heart" is not compositional; because the properties of (14) cannot be predicted given the properties of (13) or (12), it must be stored on its own.

$$MDL = \min\,[L_1(\text{G}) + L_2(\text{D}|\text{G})] \tag{8}$$

The competing demands of grammar complexity (storage or L_1) and descriptive adequacy (fit or L_2) is shown in Equation (8). The MDL paradigm aims to minimize the sum of these two terms, so that increased complexity in the grammar is only justified to the extent that it provides a better description of the data. A discovery-device grammar is in part a search problem, with the learner evaluating different chunks. Each grammar in this hypothesis space is evaluated using MDL and the best grammar is the one with the lowest MDL term. For example, this approach has been used in morphology to determine the best segmentations of words and morphs (Goldsmith, 2001, 2006; Kohonen, Virpioja, & Lagus, 2010).

$$L_C(X^n) = log_2 P(X^n) \tag{9}$$

In order to implement MDL, however, we must quantify both L_1 and L_2 (cf., Dunn, 2018b). This is done using the concept of encoding size drawn from information theory. A finding from information theory and MDL is that the optimum encoding size is equivalent to the negative log of the probability of an item. Here we use *bits* for measuring encoding size, so that the log is calculated with base two. In practical terms, this means that more probable (hence more common) items will have a smaller encoding size. Considering a simple lexical model, if a word like "the" occurs 50k times in a corpus of a million words, its probability would be 50,000/1,000,000 = 0.05, thus having an encoding size of 4.32. But if a word like "prism" occurs only twice in the same corpus, its probability would be $2/1{,}000{,}000 = 0.000002$, thus having an encoding size of 18.93. Thus, using bits as a measure of encoding and using frequency to calculate probability means that more frequent items have a lower encoding cost, which makes them more likely to be included in the grammar.

The remainder of this section considers the complexity of the grammar (its encoding size or L_1). The encoding of a corpus given a grammar (its fit or L_2) is considered in the next section. We define a construction as a sequence of slot-constraints, allowing for lexical and syntactic and semantic constraints in each slot. In order to encode each slot, we first need to encode the type of constraint; assuming that all three constraint types are equally likely, the first portion of the encoding cost for a slot is thus $1/3 = 0.333$ or 1.58 bits.

For lexical constraints, word frequency is used to calculate encoding cost. As above, "the" costs 4.32 bits because it is quite frequent, while "prism" costs 18.93 bits because it is infrequent. The total cost is then $4.32 + 1.58 = 5.90$ for "the" and $18.93 + 1.58 = 20.51$ for "prism." For syntactic and semantic constraints, we have learned categories or word classes that include many lexical items within them. To calculate encoding size for categories we take the probability of that category, based on the total sum of all the words in the category. Thus, if a category like *<transfer>* contained words with a total frequency of 10k in the corpus, the encoding size would be $10{,}000/1{,}000{,}000 = 0.01$ or 6.64 bits.

Larger categories will contain more words and thus will be more probable. In other words, larger categories will have a lower encoding cost and be more likely to be included in the grammar. In this way, the average encoding size will be highest for lexical constraints (the most item specific) and lowest for syntactic constraints (the most general) as a function of the probability of each individual member of these categories. Rather than directly define the cost of different constraint types, this follows directly from the size and probability of each of these categories. This process is shown in Figure 11 for the construction that licenses a phrase like "reminding me of chocolate." The encoding for each construction is the sum of slot-constraint costs, here 33.29 bits. The most expensive slot is the one with a lexical constraint.

The complexity of the grammar is the total bits required to encode its constructions. In the same way, the complexity of a construction is the total bits required to encode its slot-constraints. On average, lexical constraints will cost more and syntactic constraints will cost less. The cost of any given constraint and constraint type depends on the corpus of usage that is observed during training. This is shown in Table 17, which provides examples of slot costs from the news comments corpus for each of the three constraint types. Low-cost items

Table 17 Examples of encoding cost by slot type (NC).

Lexical		Syntactic		Semantic	
Average	**17.9**	**Average**	**4.7**	**Average**	**9.5**
the	5.7	sees-realizes	2.1	think-know	2.4
to	6.6	want-need	2.4	people-folks	3.3
and	6.7	bring-carry	2.7	need-want	3.7
believe	12.0	retained-confined	4.4	loose-tied	7.8
political	12.0	france-poland	4.4	boiling-boil	7.9
state	12.0	cringing-taunting	4.5	gain-gained	8.0
dust	17.4	moron-buffoon	6.9	sesame-peanuts	13.9
engineering	17.1	chickens-rabbits	7.1	antitrust-litigation	13.9
fossil fuel	17.1	chuckle-sneer	7.0	sync-setup	13.9

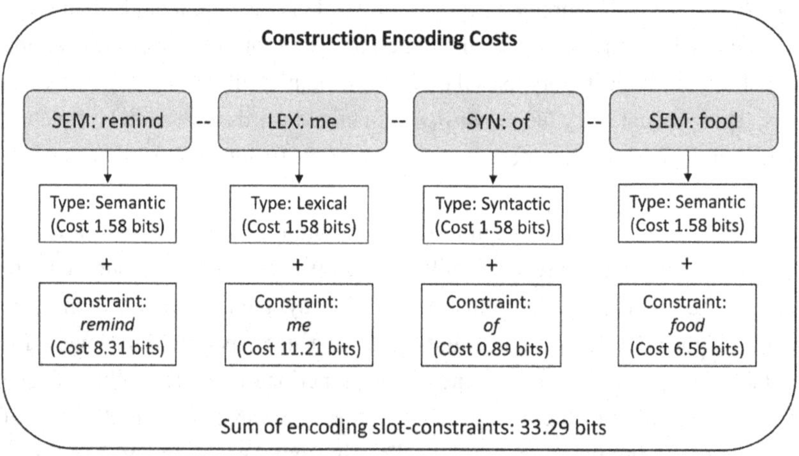

Figure 11 Encoding constructions for calculating L_1 encoding.

are at the top, medium-cost items in the middle, and high-cost items at the bottom of the table.

Table 17 shows how probability-based encoding implicitly favors more generalized constructions. The average cost of lexical items is 17.99 bits, much higher than the 4.76 bits for syntactic constraints or the 9.53 bits for semantic constraints. Within each category, however, there is still a range of encoding costs. Very common words like "the" are rather inexpensive at 5.79, while less common syntactic categories like <*chickens-rabbits*> are more expensive at 7.10. Semantic categories have the broadest range, with the common category

<think-know> costing only 2.49, while the uncommon category *<antitrust-litigation>* costs 13.91, more than many lexical constraints. These examples show how encoding cost leverages the observed probability of slot-constraints to encourage more entrenched constructions. The grammar is able to use less common basic categories as slot-constraints, but the cost of doing so is higher.

This section has presented a usage-based approach to calculating the complexity or encoding cost of a grammar by drawing on Minimum Description Length and information theory. The basic idea is that some constraints cost more to encode (thus contributing more to the complexity of the grammar) and that encoding cost is directly dependent on probability. The consequence of using MDL is that more item-specific constraints (such as lexical slots) will cost more and thus will be less likely to be included in the grammar. In other words, any construction can be learned but not all constructions are worth learning.

2.4 Grammar Fit: Probability and Encoding

We are developing a metric to determine the quality of a learned grammar. So far we have considered the L_1 term from Minimum Description Length, the cost of the grammar. The other essential component is the cost of encoding the data given the grammar. Much like perplexity for evaluating language models, this L_2 term measures the fit between the grammar and the data: How probable does the grammar consider the corpus to be? For instance, if the grammar assigns a high encoding size to a construction which ends up being quite frequent in the test corpus, the result will be a high L_2 term. This section considers how we calculate the fit between a grammar and a corpus, using bits to measure encoding size which, in turn, is derived from probabilities derived from frequencies.

Imagine that we have a grammar on hand: a set of constructions together with an empirical frequency-based encoding cost for each one. And imagine that we also have a test corpus on which to evaluate the grammar. We progress through the corpus word by word and look for the constructions in the grammar. As discussed further in Section 2.5, any sequence in the corpus which satisfies the constraints specified by a construction counts as an example or instance of that construction (a token). Thus, each time we encounter a token of a construction, we encode the corpus using a *pointer* to the construction in the grammar. Because constructions are potentially overlapping, for example (12) through (14), each with a different level of abstraction, a sequence in the corpus may be encoded using multiple pointers to different constructions.

$$L_2 = \sum pointerCosts + \sum regretCosts \tag{10}$$

We thus have two challenges: first, to calculate the pointer cost for each construction and, second, to calculate the REGRET or error in the model: parts of the corpus which are covered by no construction in the grammar. Using the test corpus, we find the frequency of each construction. The probability of each construction is then calculated as its share of the total frequency of all constructions. Thus, construction probability is relative to a specific grammar and training corpus. If a specific grammar is too small (for instance, missing many important constructions), these false negatives will inflate the probability of lesser constructions, thus altering their encoding size and providing worse generalizations to new corpora. The total L_2 measure is the sum of the bits used to encode pointers to the constructions in the grammar, where the encoding size of each pointer is calculated using probabilities from the training corpus, together with the sum of the regret or error in the model.

For any given grammar and test corpus, some parts of the corpus will not be covered, licensed, or described by a construction in the grammar. This is captured in the regret portion of the L_2 term. For each word that is not encoded, we add it to a separate regret grammar. Because each item in this regret grammar is encoded separately and because we assume no frequency information, the probability of each item is $1/total_n$. Thus, if there are 100 items in the regret grammar, the cost of each is $1/100 = 0.01$ for an individual encoding size of 6.64 (664 in total once we sum them). But if there are 1,000 items in the regret grammar, the cost of each is $1/1{,}000 = 0.001$ for an individual encoding size of 9.96 (9,960 in total once we sum them). Thus, a set of more errors also costs more individually. This cost is then doubled, once for encoding in the temporary grammar and once for encoding the pointer itself. The basic idea behind this regret calculation, then, is to penalize grammars which are inadequate to describe the test corpus: The price of false negative errors is high.

This process is shown in Figure 12, with pointer costs on the left and regret costs on the right. The cost of encoding a given corpus is the frequency of each construction multiplied by its pointer cost (its cost of usage), summed across the entire grammar. The cost of regret is the probability of a false negative error (a missing construction), with more errors leading to a higher cost per error. This cost is multiplied by the number of errors and then doubled, to account for both the pointer cost and the temporary encoding cost.

Putting the MDL metric back into context, the beam search algorithm described in Section 2.2 extracts a potential grammar from the hypothesis space. This algorithm has two thresholds: a ΔP threshold for adjacent slot-constraints and a frequency threshold for overall chunk frequencies. This MDL metric is used to evaluate a grid-search across these two thresholds in order to find those parameters which provide the best mix of memory and computation

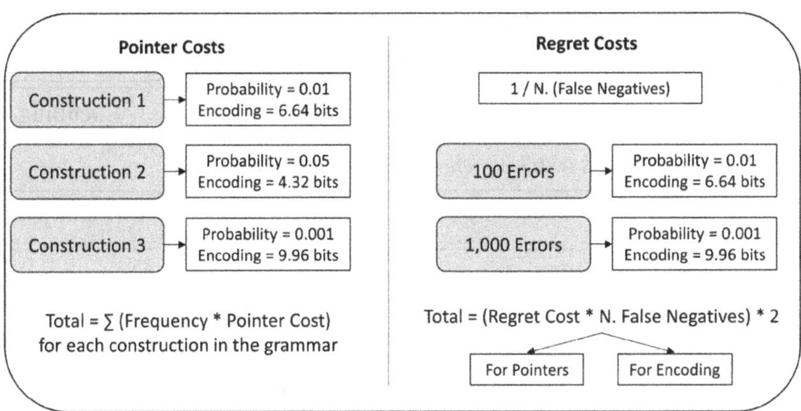

Figure 12 Encoding pointers and errors for calculating L_2 encoding.

for a particular corpus. The best grammar within this search space is the one which minimizes the sum of the L_1 and L_2 terms.

From a usage-based perspective, the types of constructions identified in this way will depend on the size of the training corpus. In other words, larger corpora will require more bits to encode in the same way that larger or more complex grammars will require more bits. Thus, larger corpora will support larger and more complex grammars. Thus, we expect that grammar size will increase as the amount of training data increases. And, further, we expect that the characteristics of constructions will change as the amount of training data increases; this is investigated further in Section 3.

We show example chunks in Table 18, together with their encoding cost, their pointer cost, and their total frequency in the test corpus. For each example, the constructional representation is displayed first; the left column provides an example of that construction (both from Wikipedia), and the following columns provide the frequency, pointer cost, and encoding cost.

At the top there is a simple syntactic construction with only two slots. This construction is quite frequent so that its pointer cost is low (6.96 bits). Because there are only two slots and both of these are defined using the less expensive syntactic constraints, the encoding cost of the construction (its contribution to grammar complexity) is only 0.66. This can be contrasted with the longer and less frequent chunk in the fourth row, with the example "something needs to." This chunk is less frequent as well as more complex, with a pointer cost of 9.60 bits and an encoding cost of 2.72 bits.

The center examples contain a mix of slot constraints: for example, the fifth row with the example "happens to remove" contains both semantic and syntactic constraints. This chunk is relatively infrequent and contains more costly

Table 18 Examples of both pointer cost and encoding cost for representative constructions.

	Example	Freq.	Pointer	Encoding
1	[SYN:68 *he-who* > SYN:219 *would-could*]			
	"he should"	5,797	6.96	0.66
2	[SEM:427 *only* > SYN:0 *contingent-establishment*]			
	"the country"	2,546	8.15	3.99
3	[LEX: "it" – SYN:47 *sees-realizes*]			
	"it reminds"	1,836	8.62	10.26
4	[SYN:68 *he-who* > SYN:30 *want-need* < SEM:10 *then*]			
	"something needs to"	932	9.60	2.72
5	[LEX: "maybe" < SYN:68 *actually-always* > LEX: "need" < LEX: "to"]			
	"maybe they need to"	3	17.88	29.91
6	[SEM:53 *goes-comes* < SEM:10 *then-once* > SYN:10 *placate-deprive*]			
	"happens to remove"	4	17.46	10.63
7	[LEX: "given" < SEM:427 *only* > LEX: "chance" < SEM:10 *then*]			
	"given the chance to"	4	17.46	29.47
8	[LEX: "a" > LEX: "fraction" < LEX: "of" < SEM:427 > LEX: "price"]			
	"a fraction of the price"	3	17.88	46.77

slot-constraints, so that its pointer cost is higher (17.46) and its encoding cost is slightly higher as well (10.63). In the final construction, with the example "a fraction of the price," we see an item-specific lexical chunk. This chunk has a similar frequency as the previous construction, so that there is a similar pointer cost of 17.88 bits. However, lexical constraints are more costly and this chunk contributes a very high 46.77 bits to grammar complexity. These examples show the application of the MDL metric to actual chunks derived from Wikipedia.

This section has considered the problem of calculating the fit between a grammar and a corpus, including both true positive attestations (pointer costs) and false negative errors (regret costs). As before, frequency in the training corpus is used to predict costs in the grammar. The basic idea behind this model is that, in usage-based grammar, any construction could be learned but not all constructions are equally worth learning. Here this is operationalized as the trade-off between memory and computation. For instance, costly item-specific constructions may be useful if they prevent false negative errors or describe an irregular form that is entrenched in its own right. But the many possible item-specific chunks will, on the whole, be discarded because of their large contribution to grammar complexity.

2.5 Parsing Corpora: True and False Positives

Parsing a construction grammar differs from other parsing problems in computational linguistics because any given span could be represented by multiple constructions. For phrase structure grammars, on the other hand, we can assume that there is one set of boundaries between each syntactic unit, even if a smaller unit is nested within a larger unit. For example, the sentence in (15) could receive the constituent parse notated with brackets in (16). At the top level, there are three units: a noun phrase, a verb phrase, and an adverb phrase. The verb phrase contains within it two sub-constituents, both noun phrases. Because a phrase structure grammar would be converted into binary Chomsky Normal Form, each parsing action involves merging two units into one: For example, "the neighbours" would be merged into a NP given the following rule: *NP -> DET N*.

(15) "The neighbours gave me a hand with the car yesterday."

(16) [NP the neighbours] [VP gave [NP me] [NP a hand]] [ADVP yesterday]

(17) [SYN: NP – SEM:*<transfer>* – SEM: *<animate>* – SYN: NP]

(18) [SYN: NP – LEX:"gave" – SEM: *<animate>* – LEX: "a hand"]

In this case, then, the parsing algorithm scans over the sentence searching for adjacent units to merge. The common CKY algorithm (cf., Grune & Jacobs, 2008) creates a parse chart by iterating over the sentence and finding all adjacent pairs which can be merged. Each merger potentially creates a new possible merger: For example, once "the neighbours" is merged into a NP, it is possible to satisfy a rule like *S -> NP VP*. The algorithm creates a chart with all possible sequences of mergers; the goal for a supervised parsing algorithm, then, is to learn from an annotated corpus which of these potential parses is most likely.

The first difference here with computational CxG is that the relevant spans are of arbitrary length, rather than constrained to sequences of only two units.

This is a part of the basic idea of CxG: “threw the ball into the crowd” and “threw the meeting into an uproar” might receive the same constituent parse but they represent, at the very least, different underlying constructions. They are different constructions because of their properties as larger units and thus must be identified as a whole.

These issues of semantics and word sense could be handled, however, using subcategorizations in the lexicon together with selectional restrictions, as in Generalized Phrase Structure Grammar (Gazdar et al., 1985). While CxG provides a motivated cognitive and psycholinguistic theory for such categorizations and constraints, even the simpler GPSG formalism could capture a good deal of the phenomena which CxG is used to describe. For example, the slot-constraints shown in the construction in (17) could also be represented using subcategorized phrase structure rules.

The larger problem has to do with levels of abstraction. There is also an idiomatic construction, represented in (18), which uses item-specific lexical constraints. The sentence in (15) thus is a token of both the generalized ditransitive construction in (17) and the idiomatic construction in (18). This kind of nesting is not simply structure within a sentence but rather structure within the grammar, in the sense that (18) is a child that inherits properties of (17). From a practical perspective, then, the parsing problem is that a sentence can have multiple parses, each identifying constructions at different levels of abstraction. The presence of one construction does not preclude the presence of another, potentially overlapping, construction.

This means that each construction is independent. Thus, as shown in the algorithm in Table 19, the basic approach is to iterate over each construction in the grammar and search for that construction in a given sentence, from left to right. First, each word in the sentence is enriched using its category memberships into a tuple representing its lexical, syntactic, and semantic values. For example, the word “neighbour” in (15) would be represented hypothetically as (LEX: “neighbor,” SYN: N, SEM: <*animate*>). These values correspond with the ontology of slot-constraints used to formulate constructions in the first place (this is hypothetical because this ontology is entirely usage based and does not assume categorizations like NOUN).[8] The algorithm then checks to see if each of the successive slot-constraints in the construction is satisfied by a particular sequence. Any constraint that is not satisfied stops that branch of the search. Stopping the search improves the efficiency of the algorithm, which is important because constructional parsing has a larger hypothesis space

[8] This stage is context free in the sense that a word is assigned to syntactic and semantic categories before it is assigned to specific constructions.

Table 19 Construction parsing algorithm.

Variables

node = slot-constraint in the input corpus
(LEX, SYN, SEM) = the domain memberships for each *node*
ConstraintType = Lexical, Syntactic, or Semantic
ConstraintValue = Specific slot-constraint
construction = a sequence of slot-constraints contained in the grammar
c_1 = starting node of construction
$[c_i \ldots c_n]$ = successor constraints in construction

Main loop

```
for each construction in the grammar:
   for each node in line:
      Categorize the (LEX, SYN, SEM) values for current word
      if c1 (ConstraintType) == node1 (ConstraintType):
         for i in construction:
            if c1 (ConstraintValue) != node1 (ConstraintValue):
               stop
            else:
               match starting at node
```

to explore. Recall that out-of-vocabulary words are assigned to the nearest syntactic and semantic word category using their character-based embedding representations, so that this algorithm is able to account for unknown words.

The output of this construction parsing algorithm is, for each construction, both the number of matches per sentence (its frequency) and the indexes of the matches. For some tasks, like enforcing the frequency constraint, only the number of matches is relevant. For other tasks, however, like calculating the regret portion of the L_2 term for MDL, we reconstruct which parts of the sentence are tokens of which constructions. Some sequences will belong to multiple constructions of different levels of abstraction, as in (17) and (18). But other sequences will be tokens of no construction and thus will constitute regret or error in the grammar, in the sense that the grammar fails to adequately describe some part of the observed usage.

(19) [SYN:150 *are* > SYN:77 *determined-permitted* < LEX: “to” > LEX: “see”]

(1) “are allowed to see”
(2) “be able to see”
(3) “am unable to see”

(4) "was unable to see"
(5) "are delighted to see"
(6) FALSE POSITIVE: "be possible to see"

We can define a TRUE POSITIVE as a token or example of a construction that has been correctly identified. This can be constrasted with FALSE POSITIVES in which the token deviates in some way from the constructional representation. Here we consider several examples of constructions from 1 million words of the news comments corpus, together with examples of false positives. For example, the construction in (19), formulated now using empirical and unsupervised slot-constraints, has the tokens in (1) through (6). These describe a complex verb phrase in which the main verb encodes a property of the agent who undertakes the action contained in the second verb. The final example differs because it is most likely an impersonal agent, as in "It will be possible to see the eclipse tomorrow." While not strictly speaking a false positive error, this example differs from the others even though it satisfies the same set of constraints.

Another example is shown in (20). This is another complex verb phrase, with the main verb encoding an evaluation of an ongoing action and the second verb falling into the usage-based category *demonstrate-conform*. The first five tokens are good examples of this construction and show the flexibility of this fully unsupervised approach to constructions. The final example, however, again does not fit necessarily with the other examples, as "exist" is a different sort of verb. While again not a proper false positive, this is an example of how the parsing of construction tokens leads to some poor examples. Similarly, the construction in (21) is a pairing of subject and verb where the subject is a pronoun of some type. The verb comes from a semantic domain of social communication, like "agree" and "support." The final example, however, is a poor fit for this construction because it has a different syntactic valency.

(20) [SYN:211 *chooses-decides* < "LEX":to > SYN:29 *demonstrate-conform*]

(1) "seeks to encourage"
(2) "tends to reflect"
(3) "choose to interpret"
(4) "continues to support"
(5) "fails to address"
(6) FALSE POSITIVE "continues to exist"

(21) [SYN:68 *he-who* > SEM:82 *considers-acknowledges*]

(1) "he engages"
(2) "she criticizes"

(3) "everyone agrees"
(4) "who supports"
(5) "nobody acknowledges"
(6) FALSE POSITIVE"who prides"

The second difference here is that usage-based computational construction grammar is necessarily unsupervised. Thus, in the beam search algorithm used to identify potential constructions, we used the ΔP association measure and a frequency measure to guide which chunks should be in the grammar. It is essential that computational CxG be unsupervised because of the PROJECTION PROBLEM (Fodor & Crowther, 2002): The grammatical exposure that a learner experiences cannot be used for positive or negative syntactic evidence until that exposure has been transformed into a potential representation. This is a serious problem for usage-based approaches to syntax. For example, even if a learner has been exposed to the generalized and idiomatic ditransitives in (15), this exposure cannot count as evidence toward either (17) or (18) unless the learner has somehow put together those potential representations. This projection problem is particularly challenging for CxG because, as noted earlier, the hypothesis space of potential constructions is larger than in other types of grammars. And the larger this hypothesis space becomes, the more difficult it is to say that a learner is aware of the particular structure it has been exposed to. Put another way, constructions cannot be observed in usage unless constructions are first hypothesized for describing that usage.

For the grammars learned here, all the structure is based on the distribution of words in a corpus. Thus, assuming that the language learner is able to identify and distinguish between distinct word-forms, these representations require only maintaining a memory of frequencies and co-occurrences. The ΔP is based on adjacent pairs, with the direction of association accounting for the degree to which one of those pairs has more or fewer possible combinations. The CBOW representations are based on the immediate surrounding context and the SG representations are based on predicting non-local context (i.e., semantic frame) given a word. In each case, our basic representations or basic constructions can be formed without intermediate syntactic representations.

2.6 Joining Shared Slots: Second-Order Constructions

In CxG, constructions are posited to exist at all levels of abstraction. For example, the lexical item in (22) could be considered a single-word construction that maps an arbitrary phonetic form to a particular set of meaning and usage. The verb phrase in (23) could also be considered a construction, a transitive verb with a specific sense of "run." And, finally, the larger verb phrase in (24), which now includes a target or destination for the verb, could also be considered a construction because it is not fully predictable given (23). We so far have learned multi-word constructions, for example the sort that would describe (23). In this section we consider a distinction between constructions at different levels of abstraction and develop an algorithm for clipping together existing constructions.

(22) run

(23) run a business

(24) run a business into the ground

In the first case, single-word constructions like lexical items or word classes are called BASIC CONSTRUCTIONS. These are learned as part of the unsupervised ontology of slot-constraints. Thus, the lexicon and the membership of distributional categories constitute our basic constructions. The next level higher, FIRST-ORDER CONSTRUCTIONS, are learned using the beam search algorithm described in Section 2.4 and evaluated using Minimum Description Length. These multi-word constructions constitute the core of the grammar. Just as in (27), however, constructions can also contain first-order constructions as their slot-constraints, resulting in larger constructions that are joined together. These are called SECOND-ORDER CONSTRUCTIONS and here we describe an algorithm that joins or merges constructions which have compatible slot-constraints.

The algorithm for clipping first-order constructions together is shown in Table 20. The basic idea is to find pairs of constructions with overlapping slot constraints: cases in which the first slot in one construction is the same as the last slot in another. In this context, *the same* means that both constructions occupy the same position in the sentence. For example, imagine that a phrasal verb construction describing a motion-event (e.g., *run into*) occurs with an animate adpositional phrase construction (e.g., *into the mayor*). These two constructions would overlap by position, whether or not the specific slot-constraints match. These overlapping constructions are joined or clipped together into a single larger construction. To avoid spurious clippings, the training corpus is then parsed and only candidates above the frequency threshold are retained. The result is a set of second-order constructions, each of which contains multiple first-order constructions as slot-fillers. Each clipping action joins two constructions. The algorithm is contained in a loop which searches for new clippings iteratively until no more are possible or until a certain number have been found (a stopping condition that improves efficiency).

Examples of second-order constructions are shown in (25) through (31). In the first case, a passive verb construction ("was selected by") is joined with a

Table 20 Construction clipping algorithm.

Variables

construction = a sequence of slot-constraints
construction[*i*] = the ith slot in construction by position
threshold = frequency threshold for new clipped constructions
newConstruction = new second-order construction
parsedCorpus = index of construction matches for corpus
parsedCorpus[*i*] = construction matches at position *i* (word-level)

Main loop

```
while True:
   clipCounter = 0
   for i in parsedCorpus:
      construction1 = parsedCorpus[i]
      for j in parsedCorpus:
         construction2 = parsedCorpus[j]
         if construction1[-1]index == construction2[0]index:
            newConstruction = construction1 + construction2[1 :]
      if freq(newConstruction) > threshold:
         add newConstruction to grammar
         clipCounter += 1
   if clipCounter == 0:
      break
```

noun phrase which provides the agent ("by the atlanta falcons"). In this case, the noun phrase is specifically restricted to a category which includes sports teams. In (26), a noun phrase that describes the orientation of a physical object ("side of") is joined with a prepositional phrase describing that object ("of the river") to produce a larger description.

(25) [SYN: *was* – SYN: *selected* – SYN: *by* – SYN: *the* –CLIP– SYN: *steelers*]
   (1) "was selected by the edmonton oilers"
   (2) "was selected by the buffalo sabers"
   (3) "was drafted by the rams"

(26) [SYN: *parapets* – SEM: *of* – SEM: *the* –CLIP– SEM: *river*]
   (1) "side of the river"
   (2) "edge of the basin"
   (3) "walls of the canal"

The example in (27) combines a declarative main clause ("i will tell you") with an additional object which transitions into a subordinate clause ("what you need to do"). In (28) a noun phrase ("a man") is joined with a relative clause which further describes that noun ("who cannot even"). In both of these cases, the valency of the original construction is increased by adding either an additional argument or subordinate material within the main phrase.

(27) [LEX: *i* – SEM: *will* – LEX: *tell* –CLIP– SYN: *you* – SYN: *what*]

(1) "i'll tell you what"
(2) "i will tell you how"
(3) "i can tell you something"
(4) "i will tell how when"

(28) [SEM: *a* – SYN: *rascal* – SYN: *who* – SYN: *wont* –CLIP– SEM: *have*]

(1) "a man who cannot even"
(2) "a lawyer who would have"

In (29) we see a declarative main clause with a verb of thinking or talking ("i saw") joined together with a complement clause with a null complementizer ("you are"). In (30) an adjective phrase ("lucky enough") is joined together with an infinitive verb phrase that describes an action ("to find"), so that the adjective describes the agent of that action. And, finally, in (31) we see an idiomatic phrase that involves an act of conspiring (whether a noun as in "collusion" or a verb as in "collude") together with the party being conspired with. This last example shows how a single construction can capture a shared meaning across different phrase structures.

(29) [LEX: *i* – SYN: *think-guess* – LEX: *you* –CLIP– SYN: *are*]

(1) "i say you are"
(2) "i think you are"
(3) "i guess you are"

(30) [SYN: *think-guess* – SEM: *enough* – LEX: *to* –CLIP– SYN: *bring*]

(1) "lucky enough to find"
(2) "smart enough to come"

(31) [SEM: *colluding* – SEM: *with* – LEX: *the* –CLIP– SYN: *foreigners*]

(1) "collude with the russians"
(2) "collusion with the russians"

These examples show cases where larger constructions are created by joining multiple existing constructions together. In order to be more precise about the level of abstractness of constructions, we distinguish between basic constructions (learned as part of the ontology of slot-constraints), first-order constructions (learned from the beam-search parsing together with grammar evaluation), and second-order constructions (learned by clipping together first-order constructions). Each of these increasingly complex structures is formed by joining together the previous layer of structure, thus modelling the emergence of constructions without innate linguistic knowledge. This idea is expanded in the next section with a focus on scaffolding constructions that contain different types of representations, so that item-specific lexical constructions are learned first and more complex syntactic constructions are learned later.

2.7 Scaffolding Structure

For a language learner, grammatical structure emerges piece by piece, bit by bit. As a result of the projection problem, more complex grammatical structures cannot be posited until simpler structures have been learned, allowing the learner to see new combinations of those simpler structures. For example, a complex second-order construction would not be visible to a learner until the previous layers (basic constructions, first-order constructions) have been learned first. We have partially modeled this by progressing from category formation to first-order constructions to second-order constructions. In this section we present a more explicit approach to the scaffolding of grammatical structure during learning. The basic idea is to repeat the underlying learning algorithm three times, each with a different set of representations: first, lexical-only constructions which make no assumptions about word classes; second, syntax-only constructions which ignore meaning-based and item-specific constraints; and third, a full construction grammar which allows all types of slot-constraints. This approach to scaffolding structure iterates over construction types of increasing complexity.

Lexical constructions (those containing only item-specific lexical constraints) will emerge before syntactic constructions in the sense that these surface-level patterns are directly observable. Syntactic constructions, on the other hand, will begin to emerge only once grammatical word classes have themselves been learned (here, after the examplar-based clustering is completed). Finally, the full grammar combines lexical, grammatical, and meaning-based constraints; this type of structure would emerge after the early rounds have been completed. We use the terms *learning* and *emerging* together, with the second term emphasizing that the grammar is not fixed once it is learned but rather is subject to change: for example, growing increasingly complex in both the number and the type of constructions it contains. In this section we compare these three stages of emergence, separating the increasingly complex constructional representations.

First, we find lexical-only constructions. These are phrases which, by definition, have only a single realization of the slot-constraints (a type–token ratio of 1). For example, a lexical-only grammar contains common prepositional phrases like (32) and common adjective-noun combinations like (33). There are also complex noun phrases (such as (34)) and common verb phrases (such as (35)). However, because this first stage of scaffolded learning has no access to word classes, the constructions are all item specific.

(32) [LEX: “across” < LEX: “the” > LEX: “river”]

“across the river”

(33) [LEX: “visual” – LEX: “artist”]

“visual artist”

(34) [LEX: “the” > LEX:“national” > LEX: “register” < LEX:“of” > LEX: “historic places”]

“the national register of historic places”

(35) [LEX: “was” > LEX: “coined” < LEX: “by”]

“was coined by”

Second, we find syntactic-only constructions based on the local CBOW embeddings. The example in (36) is a prepositional phrase indicating location in a natural environment: much like selectional restrictions, this distributional category is not simply nouns but nouns of a particular type (here, *lake, sea, water*). Similarly, (37) is a verb together with an adverbial adjunct, but with both categories defined not with abstract parts of speech so that the class of verbs is restricted (*set, worked, switched*).

(36) [SYN:252 *unique:in* < SYN:250 *unique:the* – SYN:238 *seawater-groundwater*]

(1) “in the lake”
(2) “in the sea”
(3) “in the water”
(4) “in the ocean”
(5) “in the air”

(37) [SYN:98 *generally-presumably* – SYN:196 *scrapped-switched*]

(1) "regularly set"
(2) "previously worked"
(3) "often dubbed"
(4) "ultimately switched"
(5) "previously backed"

In (38) we see a passive verb with the beginning of a prepositional phrase that specifies the agent. As before, this is formulated with verb subcategories, here verbs of writing or producing some piece of information. Similarly, the copula construction in (39) contains multiple pronouns as subject but the noun is subcategorized to include items that specify the social role of a human (*teacher*, *councilor*, *resident*). A contrast with (40) is given in (41) with a different subcategory of verb: similar constructions with non-overlapping sets of tokens.

(38) [SYN:257 *was* – SYN:61 *selected-delisted* – *syn*:149 *by*]

(1) "was released by"
(2) "was written by"
(3) "was published by"
(4) "was drafted by"
(5) "was selected by"

(39) [SYN:74 *he-she* > SYN:257 *was* – SYN:254 *a* > *syn*:206 *barrister-landowner*]

(1) "he was a teacher"
(2) "who was a servant"
(3) "he was a councilor"
(4) "he was a resident"
(5) "she was a solicitor"

(40) [SYN:17 *are* – SYN:84 *utilized-complemented* < SYN:149 *by* – SYN:250 *the*]

(1) "are owned by the"
(2) "are provided by the"
(3) "are distributed by the"
(4) "are coordinated by the"
(5) "are operated by the"

Third, the full construction grammar builds on all three types of slot-constraints in the ontology of basic constructions, forming the most complex representations. These show the first examples of semantic slot-constraints, which capture paradigmatic relationships alongside the previous syntagmatic relationships. For example, (41) represents a phrasal verb that includes all different forms of the verb *to flow*. The combination of syntactic and lexical constraints is shown in (42), a complex noun phrase which indicates players of many different sports together.

(41) [SEM:1708 *flow-flows* < SYN:124 *over-through*]

(1) "flowing from"
(2) "flow through"
(3) "flows into"
(4) "overflow from"
(5) "flows across"

(42) [SYN:197 *basketball-soccer* > LEX: "player"]

(1) "football player"
(2) "ice hockey player"
(3) "soccer player"
(4) "tennis player"
(5) "basketball player"

Another combination of syntactic and semantic constraints is shown in (43), where a particular domain of adverb is modifying a particular domain of verb. Given the impersonal style required by Wikipedia, from which these constructions are learned, this construction provides a way of attributing a sentiment to a larger population than the individual author. A complex noun phrase in (44) contains all three types of constraints to indicate examples like "a species of beetle," again a construction that is particularly entrenched in the Wikipedia register. Finally, an infinitival verb phrase is represented in (45), with the semantic constraint on the main verb providing a modality that the agent tried to undertake some action. These examples show how the interaction between slot-constraints allows many different levels of grammatical description, increasing in complexity as more types of representation are included.

(43) [SYN:98 *generally-presumably* > SEM:1658 *considered-regarded*]

(1) "also known"
(2) "generally considered"
(3) "frequently cited"
(4) "widely regarded"
(5) "initially viewed"

(44) [SEM:473 *some* > SEM:308 *species* < LEX: “of” > SYN:128 *grasshopper*]

(1) “a species of beetle”
(2) “a species of orchid”
(3) “a genus of cactus”
(4) “a genus of tiger”

(45) [SEM:747 *attempting-tried* < SEM:46 *to* > *syn*:34 *throw-turn*]

(1) “unable to leave”
(2) “attempting to catch”
(3) “tried to shoot”
(4) “attempts to go”
(5) “managed to hide”

This section has presented an iterative approach to scaffolding structure in which grammars of increasing complexity are learned by including more basic constructions (i.e., slot-constraints) in the learning process. The examples discussed result from applying the same underlying algorithm to different types of input. These three grammars can then be merged into a final full CxG, providing a synthesis of constructions at different levels of abstraction. A fully recursive approach to scaffolded structure would allow new constructions to be built on top of existing constructions, so that (for example) lexical constructions could fill a single slot within a larger syntactic construction. This fully recursive model remains a problem for future work. The central challenge is to allow constructions to be bundled as a single unit that can satisfy slot-constraints in other larger constructions. On the one hand, a fully recursive approach like this would greatly expand the already large hypothesis space. On the other hand, it would increase the complexity of construction parsing as the presence of individual constructions would no longer be independent: The discovery of one construction would directly feed the presence of other constructions relying on it to satisfy a slot-constraint. This challenge thus remains outside the scope of the current Element.

3 Forming the Constructicon

Construction grammars are more than just sets of individual constructions. The grammar as a whole becomes more complex over time through both increased exposure and scaffolded structure that allows more complex constructions to be assembled. This section explores the nature of the grammar in more detail, as outlined in Figure 13. We first consider the role of new exposure on an existing grammar: The learning process is never entirely finished. In Section 3.1 we

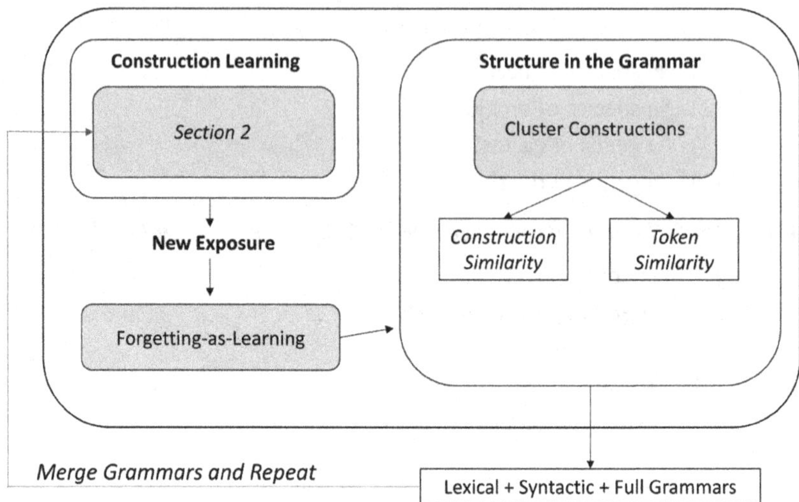

Figure 13 Cycling exposure and emergence (accumulating grammatical structure).

present a model of forgetting-as-learning which prunes constructions from the grammar over time, allowing those constructions with more productive slot-constraints to rise to the top. We then consider the nature of the grammar as the model is exposed to more data, looking at the relationship between grammar complexity and corpus size in Section 3.2. These experiments allow us to measure the impact of increased exposure on grammars as both the number of constructions and the complexity of constructions increases.

We then turn to the problem of emerging structure within the grammar itself, viewing the constructicon not as a set of individual constructions but as an interconnected network which allows both hierarchy and overlap between constructions. This constitutes a further unsupervised learning problem, organizing constructions into clusters of similar representations. First, in Section 3.3 a type-similarity approach is used to cluster related constructions together, with a focus on sequences of slot-constraints. Second, in Section 3.4 a token-similarity approach is used for the same problem, this time by finding constructions which have overlapping tokens in the corpus. These two approaches provide network structure within the grammar, producing THIRD-ORDER CONSTRUCTIONS which are composed of related first-order and second-order constructions. We complete the section by considering the implicit influence of slot-constraints across a construction (Section 3.5), by undertaking a linguistic analysis of a full construction grammar (Section 3.6), and by using type frequency to measure the productivity of constructions (Section 3.7). Because a human learner never stops being exposed to additional usage, Section 3.8 puts forward a continuous learning algorithm which cycles between exposure and emergence over time. The underlying idea in this section, then, is to learn structure within the grammar now that the previous section has focused on learning structure within individual constructions.

3.1 Forgetting for Learning: Pruning Rates

Given an initial set of exposure, computational CxG builds grammatical structure by using emerging word classes as slot-constraints (basic constructions), merging these constraints into first-order constructions and finally merging these constructions together into second-order constructions. These constructions constitute the learner's hypothesis about the productive units underlying the usage in the corpus. This hypothesis has been formed by balancing the competing demands of memory and computation, the need to include both irregular forms and predictable forms. Since constructions emerge from usage, however, this process is not constrained to a single time period: Exposure continues.

This section presents a model of forgetting during learning. The basic idea is that continued exposure allows the learner to test these hypothesized constructions and make changes as needed. In computational terms, an initial grammar is formed given exposure to a corpus, but exposure continues in the form of new subcorpora (which still represent the same population and register). For each new subcorpus, those constructions which are present are reinforced or strengthened. But those constructions which are not present are weakened and, ultimately, forgotten. This slow but steady process of forgetting brings to the fore those constructions which are the most productive, whose generalizations extend beyond the training corpus itself.

(46) [LEX: "run" – LEX: "the" – LEX: "business"]

(47) [LEX: "run" – LEX: "a" – LEX: "company"]

(48) [LEX: "run" – SYN: DET – LEX: "business"]

(49) [LEX: "run" – SYN: DET – SYN: N]

(50) [LEX: "run" – SYN: DET – SEM: *<organization>*]

The mechanism of FORGETTING allows us to differentiate between fully productive (continuously recurring) constructions and those which were only seemingly productive in the initial corpus. In this sense, forgetting is a mechanism for generalization. Consider the potential constructions in (46) through (50). Each of these is an alternate representation for the same underlying construction, licensing utterances like "run the business" or "run a company." The difference is that each captures a different level of abstraction, describing a slightly different set of utterances. The challenge for generalization is to determine which constraints capture the essential properties of this construction and which capture extraneous and forgettable noise.

Human learners have a predictable rate of forgetting cues to which they are exposed. Recent work has shown that forgetting can help word learning, in the sense that stimuli presented together with an interval of unrelated stimuli are acquired more robustly than stimuli presented in strict succession. A gap or forgetting period between sets of exposure increases retention (Vlach, 2019; Vlach & DeBrock, 2019). From a computational perspective, our construction learning algorithm is like learning from stimuli presented all at the same time. We augment this, then, with a forgetting period in which new stimuli can overwrite the previous stimuli, forcing unproductive generalizations to fall away. Once packaged into the continuous learning algorithm presented in Section 3.8, the learner is exposed to alternating periods of exposure and forgetting, the same environment which promotes human learning.

The forgetting algorithm itself is shown in Table 21 and the impact of forgetting-as-learning on the constructicon is shown in more detail in Table 22,

Table 21 Construction forgetting algorithm.

Variables

construction = a sequence of slot-constraints
weight = a weight for each construction, between 0 and 1
threshold = value below which constructions are forgotten
increment = amount to reduce weights of unobserved constructions
observationSize = amount of data, in words, to observe each iteration
observation = new corpus of exposure for forgetting and reinforcing
secondOrder = a construction made up of two merged constructions

Main loop

```
for observation in corpus[observationSize]:
    for construction in grammar:
        if construction not present in observation:
            if construction is secondOrder:
                weight = weight - (increment/2)
            else:
                weight = weight - increment
        if weight < threshold:
            remove construction from grammar
```

Table 22 Size of constructicon during forgetting, by construction type.

	Lexical-only	Syntactic-only	Full grammar
Round 1	19,188	6,179	15,397
Round 5	15,060	4,891	13,784
Round 10	11,754	3,967	12,167
Round 15	9,805	3,489	11,105
Round 20	8,619	3,168	10,437
Round 25	7,812	2,983	9,904
Round 30	7,241	2,846	9,532
Round 35	6,821	2,722	9,195
Round 40	6,465	2,637	8,965

using the Wikipedia corpus. The main loop in the algorithm iterates over new sets of exposure, parses each construction, and updates its weights accordingly. Here we use forty rounds of forgetting, each with 50k words of observation. The adjustment increment of 0.20 means that a construction must be unobserved for five successive rounds of new exposure to be forgotten (a total of 250k words). The entire forgetting stage iterates over 2 million words of exposure. Clipped constructions combine multiple existing constructions; thus, because these depend on other entrenched representations, the forgetting or decay rate for second-order constructions is half of that for first-order constructions.

The impact of forgetting-as-learning on the constructicon is shown in Table 22 using the size of the constructicon, with separate values for the lexical-only and syntactic-only and full grammars. Every fifth round of new exposure is shown as a new row. Only 33 percent of the lexical constructions remain after forgetting, 42 percent of the syntactic constructions, and 58 percent of the full constructions: This indicates that these successively more complex grammars are forming longer-lasting generalizations. In other words, the rather superficial constructions in the lexical grammar do not extend well beyond the training corpus and thus are quickly forgotten. But a majority of the constructions in the full grammar (with all three types of slot-constraints) remain after forgetting, showing that these generalizations are more robust than the surface-level lexical generalizations.

The basic idea in this section has been to interject a period of forgetting between rounds of exposure in order to reinforce the most productive constructions in the grammar. Each construction is a hypothesis about the underlying structure contained in the usage and each round of forgetting tests these individual hypotheses. Those constructions which remain productive are strengthened.

And those which are not productive are forgotten. This pushes the grammar toward deeper generalizations and away from the noise created by the large hypothesis space of potential constructions that the learner is faced with.

3.2 Acquiring Constructions: Growth of the Grammar

From a usage-based perspective, we hypothesize that grammatical structure emerges progessively given exposure to increasing amounts of usage. Given this hypothesis, we would expect that the nature of the constructicon would change in several ways as constructions become more complex and more generalized. First, we would expect that register-based differences between grammars would lessen as the amount of exposure increases: for instance, as the constructions in the grammar become more generalized, the difference between register-specific grammars would tend to reduce. Recent work has shown that this is, in fact, the case (Dunn & Tayyar Madabushi, 2021). Second, we would expect that the grammars of similar languages would have a similar growth rate given increased exposure. Other recent work has shown that this, also, is the case (Dunn, 2022a). This section focuses on our third expectation: that larger training corpora support more complex grammars.

Recall that the Minimum Description Length metric balances L_1 (grammar complexity) with its ability to describe a test corpus (L_2). In other words, greater complexity in the grammar is only justified so long as it produces a corresponding gain in the description of the corpus. The side-effect of this metric is that larger sets of exposure tend to justify or support larger grammars. The overall encoding size of a corpus of a million words will be much greater than a corpus of 250k words. A construction which occurs only a few times in the smaller corpus might not be worth including in the grammar, given the MDL metric. Yet that same construction, occuring more often in the larger corpora, may become worth including in the grammar after all. This influence of corpus size on grammar complexity is compounded by the regret component of the metric, in that eliminating a few false negative errors becomes more beneficial as the overall number of errors increases. To some degree, then, the overall size of the grammar depends on our evaluation metric.

The impact of exposure size on grammar size is shown in Table 23 for the Wikipedia register, with exposure sizes ranging from 250k words to 1 million. The number of constructions in the lexical-only, syntactic-only, and full grammars are shown both before and after the forgetting stage takes place (all exposure types use the same parameters). The size of the grammar is further divided into first-order and second-order constructions in each case. First, as expected, the size of each grammar increases with increased exposure, both

Table 23 Construction growth by numbers of constructions learned (WK).

Exposure *(Words)*	Stage *(Pruning)*	Lexical 1st	Lexical 2nd	Syntactic 1st	Syntactic 2nd	Full 1st	Full 2nd
0.25 million	Pre	4,145	75	2,742	99	6,398	1,720
	Post	3,138	67	2,057	85	5,347	1,623
0.50 million	Pre	9,127	261	4,254	152	6,534	1,255
	Post	4,994	206	2,455	122	4,665	1,111
0.75 million	Pre	13,719	464	5,228	212	9,419	2,324
	Post	5,715	269	2,492	138	5,783	1,875
1.00 million	Pre	18,504	684	5,956	223	12,093	3,304
	Post	6,165	300	2,516	121	6,510	2,455

Table 24 Change in encoding costs by exposure for the full grammar. This shows how the metric is influenced by the size of the training corpus.

Exposure	Lexical cost	Syntactic cost	Semantic cost
250k words	16.36	7.40	12.31
500k words	17.27	6.25	11.08
750k words	17.82	5.59	10.33
1 million words	18.21	5.14	9.79

before and after the forgetting stage. But the growth rate of the lexical grammar is significantly higher: Before forgetting, the first grammar contains only 22 percent of the constructions in the final grammar, compared with 46 percent for the syntactic grammar and 52 percent for the full grammar.

While the lexical grammar grows more quickly, it also loses more constructions during forgetting; the growth rate after pruning is only 50 percent. With forgetting included, the initial syntactic grammar contains 81 percent of the constructions in the final grammar and the full grammar includes 82 percent. Thus, while the MDL metric has a small influence, the size of the grammar is more dependent on forgetting. This is important because it shows that the size of the grammar is an empirical property of the observed usage, not just a side-effect of the MDL metric.

Increased exposure also has an influence on the costs of encoding different types of slot-constraints, as shown in Table 24. As the amount of exposure increases, the cost of each lexical constraint also increases, from 16.36 bits to 18.21 bits on average. At the same time, however, the cost of syntactic constraints decreases from 7.40 bits to 5.14 bits and semantic constraints from 12.31 bits to 9.79 bits. This shows how the amount of exposure also influences the nature of slot-constraints: Item-specific lexical constraints become more expensive over time and less likely to be kept in the optimal grammar. The generalizations provided by syntactic and semantic word classes, however, grow more robust so that their average cost decreases.

When taken together with previous work, the results in this section show us that the size and complexity of the grammar increases with the amount of exposure. Lexical constructions grow the most quickly but are also forgotten the most quickly. Previous work has shown that register-specific grammars become more similar given more exposure and also that the core (most frequent) constructions are learned with a relatively small amount of exposure (Dunn & Tayyar Madabushi, 2021). Other work has shown that grammars exposed only to unique individuals grow more quickly, because those individuals have their own idiosyncratic usage (Dunn & Nini, 2021). These findings combine with the changing encoding costs for each type of constraint to show that constructions grow more abstract and less item specific when the training corpus is larger. This is an important property of computational construction grammar because it models the increasing complexity of grammars in human learners as they move away from purely lexical representations (Bates & Goodman, 1997).

3.3 Networks 1: Similarity between Constructions

The focus until now has been on grammatical structure in the form of individual constructions. Thus, we have treated the constructicon as a set of constructions, albeit divided into first-order and second-order constructions (based on clipping) and lexical, syntactic, and full grammars (based on scaffolding). But what are the relationships between constructions in the grammar? There are two types of relationships to consider: first, based on similarity of constructional representations themselves (in this section) and, second, based on similarity between the tokens of constructions (in the next section).

Our basic approach to finding network relationships in the grammar, or clusters of related constructions, is to measure the pairwise similarity between constructions in order to produce a similarity matrix that can be used for clustering into construction types. The first challenge is to measure the similarity or overlap between constructions as defined by their slot-constraints. Consider the examples in (51) through (53), from the Wikipedia corpus. All three are prepositional phrases. The first two slot-constraints are shared: "of the." Our intuitions tell us that these are closely related constructions, most likely children of a more abstract “of the X” construction which, in turn, is the child of a more abstract prepositional phrase construction.

(51) [LEX: “of’ < LEX: “the” > SEM:161 *posterior-anterior*]
(1) “of the cephalon”
(2) “of the macula”
(3) “of the sternum”

(52) [LEX: “of’ < LEX: “the” > SEM:533 *diocese-archdiocese*]
(1) “of the diocese”
(2) “of the archdiocese”
(3) “of the vicariate”

(53) [LEX: “of’ < LEX: “the” > LEX: “nation”]
(1) “of the nation”

We use a sub-sequence matching algorithm to compare constructions as sequences of slot-constraints. Values closer to 1 indicate a larger number of overlapping sub-sequences and values closer to 0 indicate only a small number of overlapping sub-sequences. Slot-constraints are viewed as atomic units, so that two syntactic constraints with different values are in no way more similar than a lexical constraint and a syntactic constraint. This similarity metric is then used together with the k-medoids algorithm (used in Section 1.4 to form word categories) in order to build structure in the constructicon. This creates clusters of constructions, which we can think of as THIRD-ORDER CONSTRUCTIONS: more abstract families which contain many related first- and second-order constructions. As before, these clusters have an exemplar structure, with constructions arranged according their distance from the exemplar at the center of the cluster.

Drawing on the Wikipedia corpus, we first see a group of passive verb phrases in (54) through (57). These four constructions show how alternate slot-constraints can produce slightly different but related constructions. For example, the distinction between (54) and (55) is the subcategory of prepositions used after the passive verb. This difference is meaningful, in that “by” introduces the agent of the verb, while “as” introduces a noun phrase with a different semantic role. Thus, these constructions differ in their semantics. By contrast, (56) differs from (54) in its subcategory of main verb, each with its own behaviors, so that the construction also captures verb valency. This is extended in (57), with yet another subcategory of passive verb. These closely related constructions are thus clustered together, but remain distinguished because of their own unique meanings and valencies; taken together this is a more abstract third-order construction composed of multiple first-order constructions.

(54) [SYN:74 *he-she* > SYN: *was* – SYN:61 *selected* – SYN:149 *by* – SYN: *the*]

(1) "he was selected by the"
(2) "it was sponsored by the"
(3) "he was hired by the"
(4) "she was drafted by the"
(5) "it was chosen by the"

(55) [SYN:74 *he-she* > SYN:257 *was* – SYN:61 *selected-delisted* – SYN:209 *as*]

(1) "it was released as"
(2) "he was selected as"
(3) "he was appointed as"
(4) "she was elected as"
(5) "everything was represented as"

(56) [SYN:74 *he-she* > SYN:257 *was* – SYN:6 *superseded* – SYN:149 *by*]

(1) "it was directed by"
(2) "she was chartered by"
(3) "he was defeated by"
(4) "it was opposed by"

(57) [SYN:74 *he-she* > SYN:257 *was* – SYN:78 *admitted-asserted* – SYN:149 *by*]

(1) "he was arrested by"
(2) "he was convicted by"
(3) "he was sued by"

Another example of a type-based cluster of constructions is shown in (58) through (61). These examples represent another verb phrase, this time a main verb and an infinitive verb. In each case, the main verb represents the agent's intention in undertaking an action. This is represented by several subcategories of verb: in (58), by different members of the paradigm of "fail", in (59) by the cluster with "seeks" as its exemplar, and in (60)–(61) by the cluster with "determined" as its exemplar. There is a further semantic distinction between these constructions based on the verb in the infinitive phrase, thus bringing meaning-based differences into the distinction between constructions.

(58) [SEM:1215 *failing-failed* < SEM:46 *to* > SYN:22 *demonstrate-predicate*]

(1) "failed to identify"
(2) "failing to provide"
(3) "failed to defend"
(4) "failing to ensure"
(5) "failed to achieve"

(59) [SEM:1155 *seeks-strives* < SEM:46 *to* > SYN:22 *demonstrate-predicate*]

(1) "seeks to develop"
(2) "tries to discover"
(3) "sought to exclude"
(4) "aims to focus"
(5) "seeking to unite"

(60) [SYN:132 *determined-permitted* < SEM:46 *to* > SEM:649 *destroy-weaken*]

(1) "attempt to seduce"
(2) "attempts to reclaim"
(3) "continued to antagonize"
(4) "proposed to eradicate"
(5) "began to rebuild"

(61) [SYN:132 *determined-permitted* < SEM:46 *to* > SYN:179 *introduce-refer*]

(1) "intended to replace"
(2) "forced to marry"
(3) "refused to submit"
(4) "willing to accept"
(5) "threatened to sue"

The basic idea in this section has been that pairwise similarities between constructions can be used to build a similarity matrix for clustering related constructions together around their exemplar. A brief analysis of two such clusters shows how this adds structure to the constructicon by bringing together those constructions which are quite similar into a larger THIRD-ORDER CONSTRUCTION. Because the grammar contains constructions at all levels of abstractness, these third-order constructions are important for organizing constructions around family relationships, such as parent and child and sibling constructions. This is our first step in adding network structure to the constructicon.

3.4 Networks 2: Similarity between Tokens

Constructions may have different constraints that lead to the same set of tokens or, at least, to overlaping sets of tokens. The reason is that CxG allows constraints at different levels of abstraction, producing redundancies. For example, the constructions in (62) through (65) represent a type of spatial prepositional phrase. However, the exact formulation of constraints in these chunks leads to partially overlapping examples. In (62), there are purely item-specific constraints; in (63) the head preposition is drawn from a syntactic category; in (64) the final noun is drawn from a semantic category; and in (65) both the preposition and the head noun are defined using larger categories. From a usage-based perspective, any of these constructions could be entrenched – either because of idiosyncratic behaviors or because of frequency. Thus, we cannot rule out overlapping sets of constraints. But we do want these overlapping constructions to be grouped together in the grammar.

(62) [LEX: “at” < LEX: “the” > LEX: “bottom”]
  (1) “at the bottom”

(63) [SYN:124 *over-through* < LEX: “the” > LEX: “bottom”]
  (1) “at the bottom”
  (2) “on the bottom”
  (3) “from the bottom”

(64) [LEX: “at” < SEM:17 *a-the* > SEM:631 *top-topped*]
  (1) “at the bottom”
  (2) “at the top”

(65) [SYN:124 *over-through* < SEM:17 *a-the* > SEM:631 top-topped]
  (1) “at the bottom”
  (2) “on the top”
  (3) “from the top”
  (4) “on the bottom”
  (5) “from the bottom”

Using the same sequence-matching algorithm as before, this time applied to word-level sequences, we search for overlapping examples. For instance, all four constructions here share the example “at the bottom” even though their other examples differ. We take the highest match across all examples, so that in effect these constructions are viewed as having at least one shared token. This token-based similarity matrix is then used to cluster related constructions. Fuzzy matches are supported by requiring an overlap of 0.75 to count as a match, so that the tokens need not be exactly the same to count as overlapping. During clustering, groups of constructions which are mostly empty (i.e., with only two members) are merged into a single category. Also at this point, constructions which have completely overlapping tokens (i.e., cases where slightly different slot-constraints produce the same tokens) are merged into a single construction.

The first cluster of examples, in (66) through (69), describes noun phrases involving a governmental entity. In (66) the syntactic constraint on the head noun makes these country-level entities, while in (67) the same construction is presented with states within the US. A similar set of constraints is found in (68), but the head noun is left open; this allows a wider variety of items to fill the first slot, showing the implicit relationships between slot-constraints (cf., Section 3.5). Finally, in (69) a different form is taken, this time with non-governmental entities (like "species" or "groups") within an official area. These examples show the impact of the fuzzy matches allowed, where the two tokens being compared do not need to exactly overlap.

(66) [SYN: *the* > SYN:214 *delegation* < SYN: *of* – SYN:41 *poland-hungary*]

(1) "the council of europe"
(2) "the united states of america"
(3) "the parliament of finland"
(4) "the government of denmark"

(67) [SYN: *the* > SYN:214 *delegation* < SYN: *of* – SYN:171 *missouri-arkansas*]

(1) "the state of oregon"
(2) "the republic of texas"
(3) "the state of colorado"

(68) [SYN: *the* > SYN:214 *delegation* < SYN: *of* < SYN: *the*]

(1) "the council of the"
(2) "the summit of the"
(3) "the assembly of the"
(4) "the elections of the"
(5) "the sovereignty of the"

(69) [SYN:126 *localities-portions* – SYN: *in* < SYN: *the* > SYN:214 *delegation*]

(1) "stations in the united states"
(2) "districts in the state"
(3) "species in the united states"

(4) "dioceses in the united states"
(5) "groups in the senate"

The second example of token-based construction clusters is shown in (70) through (73). These examples are generic phrasal verbs, each with a specific verb (a lexical constraint) and a generic preposition (a semantic constraint). The token overlap here comes from the same prepositions in the same positions. This type of third-order construction, then, joins together individual phrasal verbs into a generic or more abstract phrasal verb construction.

(70) [LEX: "went" < SEM:46 *out-from*]

(1) "went out"
(2) "went to"
(3) "went from"
(4) "went straight"
(5) "went back"

(71) [LEX: "taken" < SEM:46 *out-from*]

(1) "taken at"
(2) "taken from"
(3) "taken to"
(4) "taken out"
(5) "taken back"

(72) [LEX: "returned" < SEM:46 *out-from*]

(1) "returned to"
(2) "returned from"
(3) "returned when"

(73) [LEX: "moved" < SEM:46 *out-from*]

(1) "moved to"
(2) "moved from"
(3) "moved back"
(4) "moved out"

Now that we have examined instances of both approaches to clustering constructions, we see that these clusters provide more generic or generalized representations, each with many children that are specific first-order or second-order constructions. We use the intersection of both type-based and token-based clusters to organize the grammar. In practice, this means that type-based clusters are formed first and then subdivided into token-based subclusters. This provides two tiers of family structure in the grammar.

Table 25 Number of families of constructions (third-order). *Large* clusters are type based and represent a higher-order generalization; *small* clusters are token based and represent sub-clusters within the type-based families.

	Lexical-only		**Syntactic-only**		**Full grammar**	
	Large	*Small*	*Large*	*Small*	*Large*	*Small*
BL	17	194	15	161	90	1,008
NC	18	198	18	164	110	1,325
EU	39	529	20	264	111	953
PG	19	242	16	146	107	922
PR	24	283	13	148	72	833
OS	20	280	16	180	84	847
TW	16	150	11	95	76	946
WK	25	341	15	174	45	724

The number of larger type-based families (*Large*) and smaller token-based sub-families (*Small*) is shown for each register-specific grammar in Table 25. For instance, the full grammar from the blog corpus contains 90 large families and just over a thousand sub-families. There are fewer families (and thus a less diverse range of constructions) on Wikipedia with 45 families and 724 sub-families. These third-order constructions provide a higher level of generalization. For example, the individual phrasal verbs in (70) through (73) and the individual infinitival phrases in (58) through (61) capture constructions at a higher level of abstraction. With each additional accumulation of structure, the constructicon is emerging from the bottom up, here with structure taking the form of network relationships within the grammar.

3.5 Emergent Constraints: Implicit Influences of Slot-Fillers

The grammar contains constructions that are sequences of slot-constraints, where each constraint is itself a basic-level construction. On their own, these basic-level constructions can be analyzed according to their syntactic and semantic properties, as was done in Section 1. Once combined with other slot-constraints, however, these basic constructions can take on new and emergent properties that they did not exhibit in isolation. In other words, there is a sort of coercion across slots in a single construction so that the grammatical description it provides is not a simple sum of its parts. There is an indirect influence beween slot-constraints, then, so that for example not all members of a category satisfy the implicit joint constraints of a construction. This section examines several constructions derived from the Project Gutenberg corpus to show the influence that these implicit relationships between slot-constraints can exert.

We start with a comparison of (74) and (75), both containing the same syntactic slot-constraint marked in bold (162). In (74) this constraint appears as a relative pronoun but in (75) it appears as the first-person plural pronoun. Thus, in this case the same underlying basic construction takes on a different form when synthesized with the other slot-constraints in the construction. In other words, the slot-constraint in isolation does not always predict its emergent behaviors in a first-order construction.

(74) [LEX: "those" – SYN:**162** – SYN:183 *guessed-remembered*]

(1) "those who understood"
(2) "those who knew"
(3) "those who thought"
(4) "those who heard"
(5) "those who wrote"

(75) [SYN:**162** – SYN:85 *wont-could* – SEM:1448 *understand* – SEM:0 *that*]

(1) "we shall understand it"
(2) "we must recognize that"
(3) "we may understand that"
(4) "we shall speak more"

The examples in (76) and (77) show the implicit influence in a main-verb slot-constraint. In the first case, (76), the syntactic constraint in bold is an active verb indicating motion toward something, with examples like "started" and "ran" and "rushed." Yet in the second case, (77), the same constraint is in a different constructional frame and appears as "struck" and 'stopped" and "smashed." The previous constraint of interest (162) also appears here again, but with yet another form ("have"). Thus, the exact properties of each basic construction, via coersion, depend to some degree on the other constraints in the construction. For instance, this is how the long-distance SEM constraints take on a certain degree of grammatical information as well.

(76) [SYN:**216** ***stumped-shoved*** – SYN:173 *into* – SEM:380 *the* – SEM:360 *road*]

(1) "went into the park"
(2) "started toward the bridge"
(3) "ran along the trail"
(4) "rushed at the bridge"

(77) [SYN:85 *wont-could* – SYN:162 – **SYN:216 *stumped-shoved***]

(1) "would have struck"
(2) "should have gone"
(3) "might have stopped"
(4) "would have smashed"

In (78) the semantic constraint (2041) serves as an all-purpose auxiliary verb, for example appearing as "will" and "cannot." In (79), however, this same constraint appears only as the infinitival "to." This is another example of the different degrees of flexibility shown by slot-fillers.

(78) [SEM:**2041** – SEM:953 *constrain-allow*]

(1) "will dictate"
(2) "would impose"
(3) "may embrace"
(4) "cannot compel"

(79) [SEM:2204 *endeavor* – SEM:**2041**]

(1) "endeavour to"
(2) "strive to"
(3) "undertake to"
(4) "strives to"

A final example, this time involving nouns encoded by a semantic constraint, is shown in the contrast between (80) and (81). In the first instance, the semantic domain 2114 appears as "door" and "window" because the construction is encoding movement toward an interior location on a horizontal plane. In the second instance, however, the construction as a whole is encoding movement on a vertical plane, so that the same semantic constraint appears in the form of "stair" and "stairs." Here, again, the specific behavior of a slot-constraint is produced via coersion given its relationship with the other slot-constraints.

(80) [SEM:64 *turned* – SYN:173 *into* – *sem:380 the* –*CLIP*– SEM:2114 **door**]

(1) "went toward the door"
(2) "moved toward the door"
(3) "turning from the window"
(4) "looked from the window"
(5) "pointed toward the doorway"

(81) [SYN:146 *up* – SEM:380 *the* – SEM:2114 **door**]

(1) "down the stairs"

(2) "on the stairs"
(3) "up the stairs"
(4) "up the stair"
(5) "on the stair"

This section has looked at examples of emerging constraints within a construction which arise as a product of coercion or relationships between slot-constraints. The basic idea is that, once embedded within a larger construction, the behavior of a basic construction conforms to its larger unit. This was seen across pronominal forms, verbs, auxiliary verbs, and nouns. Having analyzed this final attribute of constructional representations, we turn in the next section to an analysis of the constructicon itself from a linguistic perspective.

3.6 Analyzing the Constructicon

Now that we have walked through the stages of learning a constructicon that represents a particular population and register, we undertake a linguistic analysis of selections of that constructicon. This constitutes an analysis of the final output of computational CxG. In this case, we draw from the grammar representing Project Gutenberg. We start with prepositional constructions and then look at examples of nominal, verbal, and then clause-level constructions.

Starting in (82), we see a second-order prepositional construction, or rather a complex noun phrase clipped together with a prepositional phrase. This is not a generic phrase structure prepositional phrase, as it is specific to a location which can be surrounded. A more item-specific example from the same cluster is shown in (83), here confined to locations in the home or house. Thus, this construction is related to interior locations. Finally, in (84) we see a prepositional phrase proper, here confined to a specific sense of "up" and "down" in which the head noun is restricted to that class which is traveled by going "up" or "down": a river, a lake, a valley, etc. These examples show how constructions maintain elements of meaning in their grammatical representations.

(82) [SEM:380 *a-the* – SYN:63 *parapets* – SEM:6 *of* – LEX: "the" *–CLIP–* SYN:225 *courtyard*]

(1) "the edge of the bench"
(2) "the side of the fireplace"
(3) "the ditches of the castle"
(4) "the ground of the mezzanine"
(5) "the walls of the room"

(83) [SEM:380 *a-the* – SYN:63 *parapets* – SEM:6 *of* – LEX: "the" – SEM:2167 *parlour*]

(1) "the walls of the room"
(2) "the wall of the house"
(3) "the windows of the house"
(4) "the ceiling of the room"

(84) [SYN:146 *up-down* – SEM:380 *a-the* – SEM:325 *river-headwaters*]

(1) "up the river"
(2) "down the river"
(3) "up the valley"
(4) "down the valley"
(5) "up the lake"

We look at two simple examples of nominal constructions in (85) and (86). Both are defined with a lexical constraint "the" plus a head noun. But rather than a meaningless phrase structure rule, the class of nouns here is specified using a semantic constraint: in the first case, ships and, in the second case, horses. Because nominal constructions like this are used to formulate larger verbal constructions, for instance, these distinctions are necessary for formulating selectional restrictions within larger verbal constructions.

(85) [LEX: "the" – SEM:715 *schooner-brig*]

(1) "the whaler"
(2) "the schooner"
(3) "the steamer"
(4) "the sloop"
(5) "the frigate"

(86) [LEX: "the" – SEM:722 *horse-mule*]

(1) "the horse"
(2) "the pony"
(3) "the stallion"
(4) "the mule"
(5) "the mare"

Three examples of active verb phrases are shown in (87) through (89). Each consists of the main verb plus the beginning of a prepositional phrase. In the first case, we see how semantic constraints can capture paradigmatic relationships, here with different forms of the verb "to roll". And we also see how the choice of preposition is verb-specific, in the sense that this use of "roll" is up or down. In (88) we see another example of a paradigmatic constraint, with different forms of "to fly". The choice of prepositions is much wider, however, so that this is not constrained to one sense of the verb. Finally, in (89) we see a more item-specific construction from the same cluster, here with different forms of "leap" together with a preposition like "into". This verbal construction thus indicates the valency of the main verb and would be clipped directly with nominal constructions indicating the target location.

(87) [SEM:219 *rolled* – SYN:146 *up-down* – SEM:380 *a-the*]

(1) "rolled up the"
(2) "rolling on the"
(3) "rolled down the"
(4) "roll up the"

(88) [SEM:339 *flying-fly* – SYN:173 *into-through* – SEM:380 *a-the*]

(1) "flying into the"
(2) "flew across the"
(3) "fly through the"
(4) "flight from the"
(5) "flew away in"
(6) "flown from the"

(89) [SEM:237 *leaping* – SYN:173 *into-through* – SEM:380 *a-the*]

(1) "leaping into the"
(2) "leap into the"
(3) "leapt into the"
(4) "leaps into the"

Three more verbal constructions are shown in (90) through (92), starting with a passive construction in (90), in the past tense. As before with verbal constructions, there is not a single class for all verbs, but classes for verbs with a similar meaning and usage. The second-order verbal construction in (91) shows a case where one sense of the verb is specified, here "walk" in different forms capturing movement relative to a location. The last example, in (92), shows a complex phrase with an infinitive object, the main verb specifying the modality with which the infinitive verb is carried out. These examples show some of the range of verbal constructions in the grammar.

(90) [SEM:1519 *would* – SYN:223 *been* – SYN:101 *assimilated*]

(1) "had been corrupted"
(2) "had been treated"

(3) "had been educated"
(4) "had been misinformed"
(5) "had been addicted"

(91) [SEM:1194 *walking* – SYN:173 *into* – lex:the *–CLIP–* SYN:225 *courtyard*]

(1) "walked towards the entrance"
(2) "walking into the town"
(3) "walked across the terrace"
(4) "walk across the garden"
(5) "walked round the house"

(92) [SYN:133 *determined* – SEM:2041 *will-to* – SYN:235 *carry* – LEX: "up"]

(1) "determined to make up"
(2) "willing to give up"
(3) "tried to make up"
(4) "decided to give up"
(5) "trying to conjure up"

The last set of examples, in (93) through (96), represent clause-level constructions that go beyond an immediate verb phrase. In (93) we see a comparative copula phrase with a range of comparative adjectives. In (94) there is an expletive subject "it", a sort of filler that actually introduces an impersonal verb phrase. Similarly, the example in (95) shows a conditional that begins a new clause. And, finally, in (96) there is a verb of saying or thinking that introduces a complement clause. This range of examples shows the way in which computational CxG captures clause-level structures; these could be further clipped with nominal and verbal constructions.

(93) [SEM:26 *'s-was* – SEM:1181 *larger-smaller* – LEX: "than"]

(1) "is greater than"
(2) "was bigger than"
(3) "was greater than"
(4) "was larger than"
(5) "is larger than"

(94) [SEM:0 *that-thought* – SYN:197 *wasn-weren* – SYN:162 *if-always* – SYN:133 *determined –CLIP–* LEX: "to"]

(1) "it is usually possible to"
(2) "it is now proposed to"
(3) "it is not possible to"

(4) "it is not necessary to"
(5) "it is only necessary to"

(95) [LEX: "if" – SYN:162 *if-always* – SYN:133 *determined* – SEM:2041 *will-to*]

(1) "if she meant to"
(2) "if you fail to"
(3) "if we attempt to"
(4) "if they wished to"
(5) "if she expected to"

(96) [SYN:162 *if-always* – SYN:133 *determined* –SEM:2041 *will-to –CLIP–* SEM:589 *think-know* –SEM:0 *that-though*]

(1) "always pleased to think that"
(2) "only meant to say that"
(3) "not prepared to agree with"
(4) "actually began to think that"
(5) "only began to feel that"

The discussion in this section has provided a short overview of some prepositional, nominal, verbal, and clausal constructions from the grammar derived from the Project Gutenberg corpus. Those constructions which are quite similar (such as (82)–(83) and (85)–(86) are in fact drawn from the same third-order constructions, thus showing the generalization provided by these more abstract constructions as well. While there are too many third-order constructions to examine each individually, these examples provide a representative example of the way in which constructions join together to represent grammatical structure at the sentence level.

3.7 Productivity in the Grammar

We expect that constructions within the grammar will range across the entire lexico-grammatical continuum, between item-specific constructions (more like lexical items) and schematic constructions (more like syntactic items). This is one of the core empirical facts that motivates CxG. In this section we use corpus-based measures of productivity to explore this continuum within the grammar. The main measure used here is type frequency; previously we have relied on token frequency alone for evaluating properties like entrenchment.

(97) [SEM:0 *i-even* > SYN:48 *won't* – SEM:0 *i-even* SYN:48 *won't* – LEX: "to"]

(a) "i don't even want to"
(b) "i won't try to"

(c) "i should never need to"
(d) "i would never want to"

(98) [SYN:184 *are-were* > *lex*: "supposed" < *sem* :8 *to*]

(a) "are supposed to"
(b) "were supposed to"

The idea of type frequency can be illustrated using the examples in (97) and (98). The schema or construct is the construction itself (i.e., (97) and (98). The type frequency is the number of unique examples found in a particular corpus. In this case, these constructions are drawn from the blog grammar and frequency is calculated using a 1 million word test sample from that same corpus. The first example is quite productive, with a type frequency of 125 but the second example is quite item specific with only two types per million words. Thus, type frequency in a test corpus is a measure of the productivity of individual constructions that can also be used to situate them on the continuum between grammar and lexis. High token frequency may be comprised of a large number of instances of the same construct but high type frequency shows that variations are possible within the instances or constructs of a construction.

A breakdown of grammar size and type frequency by register and level of abstractness is shown in Table 26. Each row represents a separate register, from blogs (BL) to Wikipedia (WK). The columns represent separate levels of abstractness: from first-order to third-order, which is broken into two categories based on the larger type-based clusters (*b*) and the smaller token-based clusters (*a*). The number of constructions is given under *Cxns*: for example, there are 11,467 first-order constructions in the blog register and 1,169 of the

Table 26 Productivity of constructions by register and level of abstractness using average type frequency within each category. Higher type frequencies indicate more productive constructions.

	1st-order		2nd-order		3rd-order (a)		3rd-order (b)	
	Types	*Cxns*	*Types*	*Cxns*	*Types*	*Cxns*	*Types*	*Cxns*
BL	23	11,467	15	2,858	179	1,169	1994	105
EU	13	12,999	5	404	80	1,217	740	131
NC	20	16,596	10	793	178	1,489	2072	128
OS	26	14,388	11	636	229	1,027	2350	100
PG	24	15,255	11	363	194	1,068	1688	123
PR	19	11,567	14	365	147	981	1691	85
TW	21	12,052	13	388	181	1,041	2165	87
WK	17	9,824	7	330	140	898	2099	60

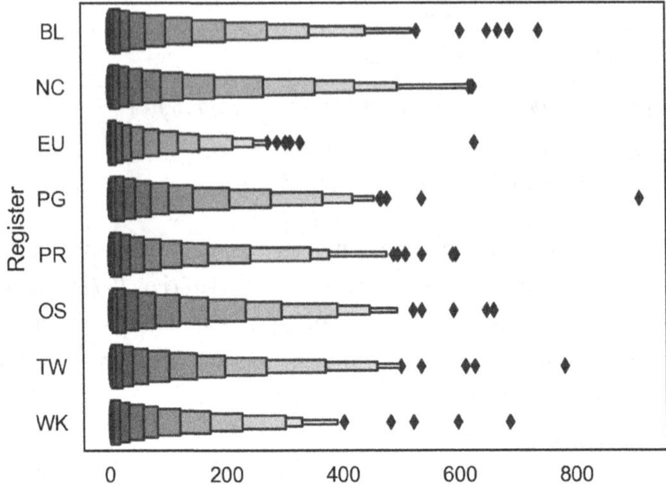

Figure 14 Distribution of type frequencies for first- and second-order constructions by register-specific grammar.

smaller type-based third-order constructions. Within each type of construction the table also shows the mean number of types per construction in a 1 million word corpus (these type frequencies are averaged across ten independent test corpora to provide a more robust estimate). What we see, then, is that first-order constructions average around 20 types per construction, while third-order constructions average around 200 and 2,000, respectively. Constructions with more types are more productive. There is a close relationship, then, between position on the lexico-grammatical continuum and productivity.

The distribution of type frequencies as a proxy for productivity is shown in Figure 14 for first- and second-order constructions (i.e., those which are sequences of slot-constraints) and for third-order constructions in Figure 15 (i.e., those which are clusters of related constructions). We can interpret this visualization as an approximation of the continuum between lexis-like constructions (on the left with lower type frequencies) and syntax-like constructions (on the right with higher type frequencies). While the mean type frequency for first-order constructions is around twenty, for example, we see that there are constructions with type frequencies of several hundred parts per million and outliers (the diamonds) with many hundreds. These constructions with more types are more schematic or syntactic in nature and there are fewer of these simply because they capture higher-order generalizations. In the same way, many third-order constructions have several thousand types per million words, again indicating a higher level of abstraction and schematicity.

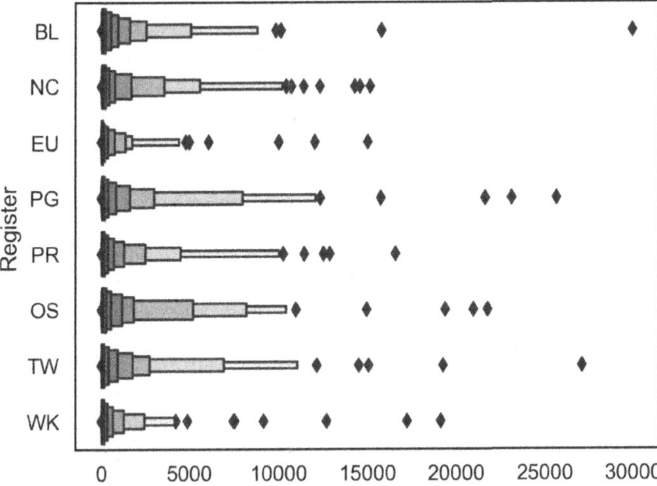

Figure 15 Distribution of type frequencies for third-order constructions by register-specific grammar.

There are two main takeaways from this section: First, the relative productivity of constructions largely corresponds with our computational distinction between first-order, second-order, and third-order constructions. Thus, this is an empirical validation of that distinction. Second, we can use corpus-based measures of productivity as a way of describing these constructions and thus as a way of organizing and exploring the constructicon itself. This is a helpful tool when the grammars contain many first-order constructions, some very item specific and others very schematic. These figures explicitly position the constructicon on the continuum between purely lexical and purely schematic representations.

3.8 Continuous Learning: Cycling Exposure and Emergence

So far we have used continued exposure to model the forgetting of constructions as a part of the learning process and built network structure between constructions in the grammar. The current model, then, takes an initial set of usage and learns the ontology of slot-constraints together with a construction grammar. Once this is complete, new exposure is used to observe the grammar, test its grammatical hypotheses, and slowly forget those constructions which fall out of usage. Thus, we have exposure for learning and exposure for forgetting. This section expands this two-part cycle into continuous grammar learning by alternating between learning and forgetting over time.

Just like a human learner, computational CxG is continuously exposed to new usage. This usage alters the background distributional patterns that reflect the learner's linguistic knowledge. Thus, the expected relationships between slot-constraints change over time. This can lead to the emergence of new constructions, which themselves constitute individual hyptheses about the grammatical structure being observed. Additional new exposure then again evaluates these new hypotheses during an additional round of forgetting: Some fail and thus are forgotten, but others pass and are reinforced. The basic idea behind the continuous learning algorithm is to alternate between the learning stage and the forgetting stage indefinitely over new subcorpora.

Thus, computational CxG captures the ACCUMULATION of grammatical structure: The more exposure, the more complex the grammar can become. At the same time, the more exposure, the more constructions are added to the grammar. While constructions can be forgotten, there is nonetheless a steady accumulation of new grammatical structures that the learner discovers.

We expect the nature of constructions, in the aggregate, to change as structure accumulates. For example, the number of lexical items will continue to grow, which means that the probability of any given lexical item will decrease. This will, in turn, increase the encoding costs of lexical constraints. On the other hand, the number of syntactic and semantic categories is fixed, although new words can be added to existing categories. Thus, we expect that item-specific constraints will become more costly over time and therefore less common; this is one way in which constructions become more generalized over time.

The continuous learning algorithm itself is shown in Table 27. This is a simple iterating algorithm, alternating between learning aand forgetting as new

Table 27 Continuous learning algorithm.

Variables
observationSize = amount of data to observe each iteration
observation = new corpus of exposure
grammar = existing set of constructions
newGrammar = current set of constructions
learnConstructions = construction learning algorithm
Main loop
for observation in corpus[observationSize]:
newGrammar = learnConstructions(observation):
if grammar present:
grammar = merge(grammar, newGrammar

Table 28 Construction growth during continuous learning by total number of constructions (PG).

Learning round	Lexical		Syntactic		Full	
	1st	2nd	1st	2nd	1st	2nd
Cycle 1	3,975	7	2,389	37	12,881	1,332
Cycle 2	4,231	8	2,583	48	16,296	1,774
Cycle 3	4,349	7	2,656	49	17,641	2,034
Cycle 4	4,399	10	2,723	60	18,686	2,287
Cycle 5	4,456	11	2,755	67	19,204	2,347
Final	**3,657**	**8**	**2,435**	**62**	**17,001**	**1,954**

usage is encountered. Constructions from a previous grammar are forgotten at half the rate of newly learned constructions, which means that constructions become more entrenched the more cycles of continuous learning they go through.

The accumulation of constructions during continuous learning is shown in Table 28 for the Project Gutenberg corpus. The size of the constructicon is divided into the three layers of grammars (lexical-only, syntactic-only, and full) as well into first-order and second-order constructions within each. The final round, shown here in bold, forgets constructions but does not learn any new representations. This final additional forgetting round ensures that the most recently learned constructions are not overly favored.

Table 28 shows that continuous learning has little influence on the overall size of lexical and syntactic grammars: These are almost the same size at the end of the five cycles of learning and forgetting. In fact, lexical constructions are even reduced after the final forgetting stage, so that there are fewer at the end than after the first round. The full grammar, however, shows a very different pattern: Continuous learning here accumulates more representations with each additional round. The final grammar contains 33 percent more constructions than the first-round grammar. This indicates that the lexcal and syntactic constructicons reach their limit while the more diverse representations in the full constructicon continue to expand given new exposure. The purpose of this section has been to explore the impact of a continuous learning algorithm in which the grammar continues to be exposed to new usage. For the full grammar, containing more complex constructions, this leads to a steady accumulation of structures.

4 Conclusions

4.1 Learnability, Variability, and Confirmability

Construction Grammar is a usage-based approach to syntax in which a core theoretical concept, the CONSTRUCTION, maps between form and meaning at different levels of abstraction. The advantage of this construction-based approach to syntax is that it provides a robust description of language acquisition (Goldberg, 2006), linguistic variation (Dunn, 2018a, 2019b), figurative meaning (Sullivan, 2013), and ultimately the productive capability of grammar itself (Goldberg, 2019). The disadvantage is that, given the rich representations used for constructions, the hypothesis space of potential grammars is much larger than in other approaches to syntax. At the same time, CxG insists that language must be learned in a usage-based fashion without innate structure that is specific to language itself. The combination of these two facts creates a major challenge: CxG aims to describe more than do other syntactic paradigms while assuming less about the language faculty.

The challenge, then, is to provide a theory of CxG that lives up to this joint requirement of rich hypothesis spaces with no starting knowledge. It is absolutely clear that a knowledge-based or introspection-based approach to computational CxG is inherently inadequate. First, the concept of entrenchment is a relationship between a particular construction and a particular population using a particular register. This is a fundamentally empirical notion. Second, a reliance on introspection undercuts any claims about learnability and innateness: The linguist doing the analysis has already learned the language and with their own knowledge in the loop we could never test how much knowledge is, in fact, required to produce a construction grammar. Third, we must take seriously the projection problem, in which usage does not constitute exposure until some initial intermediate analysis is available (i.e., emerging structure). In short, until a syntactic analysis has taken place it is impossible for the learner to even count the frequency of different structures. A reliance on introspection and knowledge representation eliminates any hope of answering our starting questions about the learnability, variability, and confirmability of construction grammars.

The only solution, then, is to view a construction grammar as a discovery-device grammar which predicts a constructicon given a corpus of usage while assuming no specific linguistic structures to start with, not even simple distinctions between nouns and verbs. A computational construction grammar is not a specific constructicon, in other words, a specific set of grammatical annotations; it is rather a means of predicting a constructicon (emerging structure) given a corpus (exposure). The universal grammar of this approach does not

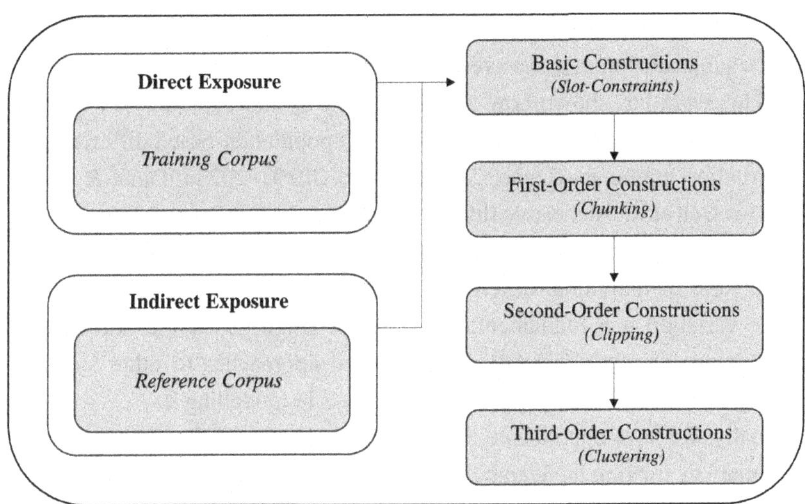

Figure 16 Emergence of constructions (layers of increasing complexity).

contain specific structures but rather the learning mechanisms which create those structures, which in this case can be defended as general non-linguistic abilities. The increasing complexity of constructions from this perspective is schematized in Figure 16, in which exposure leads to slot-constraints and word classes (basic constructions), which are formed into sequences of slot-constraints via chunking (first-order constructions) and then merged by clipping into larger sequences (second-order constructions). Finally, clustering based on network structure in the grammar produces more abstract families of related constructions (third-order constructions), thus modeling hierarchy within the grammar.

This work directly confronts the problem of *learnability*, which is the basic question of whether the rich representations of CxG can be acquired without starting structure. As argued in Section 1.7, computational CxG is uniquely situated to evaluate the question of learnability because of the ability to strictly demarcate the amount and the source of exposure. While computational work remains disconnected from participant-based studies, this work does tell us a great deal about the emergence of structure at scale: across the entire grammar, across many participants, and, in related work, across many languages (Dunn, 2022a). This scale is impossible to achieve in laboratory studies, confined to a small number of conveniently available participants.

At the same time, this work provides insight into the problem of *variability* in construction grammars. Unlike traditional grammars, the usage-based CxG paradigm views a grammar as entrenched constructions, where entrenchment is fundamentally related to exposure. This means that CxG predicts that grammars will be subject to variation as a result of differences in exposure between learners. This work has shown how grammars vary by their amount of exposure. Related work has shown that there are robust population-based differences in construction grammars (Dunn, 2018a, 2019b, 2019c, 2023a; Dunn & Wong, 2022) as well as register-based differences (Dunn, 2022a; Dunn & Tayyar Madabushi, 2021). Recent work has even shown the impact of individual exposure in the form of individual differences in the grammar (Dunn & Nini, 2021). While variation is a fundamental property of language, neither knowledge-based approaches to CxG nor computational approaches to other syntactic paradigms have had nearly this level of success in modelling it.

Finally, we have approached the problem of *confirmability* of construction grammars by treating the learned constructicon as a hypothesis which can then be evaluated by quantitative means but also by the intuitions of linguists. By removing introspection from the formation of grammars, we make it possible to apply introspection to analyze learned constructions without thereby causing a circular line of reasoning. Computational CxG is, in this sense, both replicable and falsfiable.

4.2 Remaining Challenges

The basic idea here, then, has been to show that a truly usage-based syntax is, in fact, possible. In spite of the many advances represented here, however, many problems still remain. In particular, much work needs to be done on recursion, semantics, morphology, unfilled slots, and dependency structures in usage-based computational CxG.

First, a fully recursive approach to CxG would allow any construction, once learned, to potentially satisfy a slot-constraint in a first-order or second-order construction. This is not currently implemented; clipping is a partially recursive method in which first-order constructions can only fill slots at the edges of another construction.

Second, distributional semantics for a construction grammar also remains unimplemented. This would likely proceed, for example, by adapting a self-supervised language model (such as the CBOW and SG models used to form word classes) to observe the occurrence and co-occurrence of constructions. This would produce a vector representation for constructions in much the same way that current models produce vector representations for individual words.

Third, while the basic constructions used here do provide a simplistic separation between syntagmatic and paradigmatic relationships between words, this work does not delve into a representation of constructional morphology. From a theoretical perspective, we would expect a symmetry between the emergence of constructions in syntactic structure and in morphological structure.

Fourth, the slot-constraints here vary in their level of abstractness (from lexical to semantic constraints), where a more abstract constraint has a larger and more heterogeneous range of fillers. What remains absent, however, is the use of completely unfilled slots to allow the representation of non-continguous constructions. Such an unfilled slot would allow the presence of an unspecified set of other constructions to be placed within a matrix construction. While important for representing many syntactic phenomena, this remains unimplemented in this work.

Fifth, we have viewed a construction as a sequence of slot-constraints, in part inspired by an underlying phrase structure grammar. However, we could also have viewed constructions as slot-constraints arranged by dependency relationships rather than linear order, specifying head-dependent relationships between slots. There is no theoretical reason why CxG could not be built on top of a dependency grammar and this remains a challenge for future work.

References

Bates, E., & Goodman, J. (1997). On the inseparability of grammar and the lexicon: Evidence from acquisition, aphasia and real-time processing. *Language and Cognitive Processes*, *12*(5–6), 507–584. https://doi.org/10.1080/016909697386628.

Bengio, Y., Ducharme, R., Vincent, P., & Jauvin, C. (2003). A neural probabilistic language model. *Journal of Machine Learning Research*, *3*, 1137–1155.

Beuls, K., & Van Eecke, P. (2023). Fluid construction grammar: State of the art and future outlook. In *Proceedings of the First International Workshop on Construction Grammars and NLP (CxGs+NLP, GURT/SyntaxFest 2023)* (pp. 41–50). Washington, DC Association for Computational Linguistics. https://aclanthology.org/2023.cxgsnlp-1.6.

Biber, D., & Conrad, S. (2009). *Register, genre, and style*. Cambridge University Press.

Bouma, G. (2009). Normalized (pointwise) mutual information in collocation extraction. In *Proceedings of the German Society for Computational Linguistics and Language Technology* (Vol. 30, pp. 31–40). Gunter Narr Verlag.

Brysbaert, M., Warriner, A., & Kuperman, V. (2014). Concreteness ratings for 40 thousand generally known English word lemmas. *Behavior Research Methods*, *46*, 904–911. https://doi.org/10.3758/s13428-013-0403-5.

Burdick, L., Kummerfeld, J. K., & Mihalcea, R. (2021). Analyzing the surprising variability in word embedding stability across languages. In *Proceedings of the 2021 Conference on Empirical Methods in Natural Language Processing* (pp. 5891–5901). Association for Computational Linguistics.

Chen, S., & Goodman, J. (1999). An empirical study of smoothing techniques for language modeling. *Computer Speech and Language*, *13*, 359–394.

Church, K., & Hanks, P. (1990). Word association norms, mutual information, and lexicography. *Computational Linguistics*, *16*(1), 22–29. https://doi.org/10.3115/981623.981633.

Devlin, J., Chang, M.- W., Lee, K., & Toutanova, K. (2019). BERT: Pre-training of deep bidirectional transformers for language understanding. In *Proceedings of the 2019 Conference of the North American Chapter of the Association for Computational Linguistics: Human Language Technologies, volume 1 (long and short papers)* (pp. 4171–4186). Association for Computational Linguistics. https://doi.org/10.18653/v1/N19-1423.

Doumen, J., Beuls, K., & Van Eecke, P. (2023). Modelling language acquisition through syntactico-semantic pattern finding. In *Findings of the Association for Computational Linguistics: EACL 2023* (pp. 1347–1357). Association for Computational Linguistics.

Dunn, J. (2010). Gradient semantic intuitions of metaphoric expressions. *Metaphor and Symbol*, *26*(1), 53–67. https://doi.org/10.1080/10926488.2011.535416.

Dunn, J. (2013). How linguistic structure influences and helps to predict metaphoric meaning. *Cognitive Linguistics*, *24*(1), 33–66. https://doi.org/10.1515/cog-2013-0002.

Dunn, J. (2017). Computational learning of construction grammars. *Language & Cognition*, *9*(2), 254–292.

Dunn, J. (2018a). Finding variants for construction-based dialectometry: A corpus-based approach to regional CxGs. *Cognitive Linguistics*, *29*(2), 275–311.

Dunn, J. (2018b). Modeling the complexity and descriptive adequacy of construction grammars. In *Proceedings of the Society for Computation in Linguistics* (pp. 81–90). Association for Computational Linguistics.

Dunn, J. (2018c). Multi-unit directional measures of association moving beyond pairs of words. *International Journal of Corpus Linguistics*, *23*(2), 183–215.

Dunn, J. (2019a). Frequency vs. association for constraint selection in usage-based construction grammar. In *Proceedings of the Workshop on Cognitive Modeling and Computational Linguistics* (pp. 117–128). Association for Computational Linguistics.

Dunn, J. (2019b). Global syntactic variation in seven languages: Toward a computational dialectology. *Frontiers in Artificial Intelligence*, *2*(15). https://doi.org/10.3389/frai.2019.00015.

Dunn, J. (2019c). Modeling global syntactic variation in English using dialect classification. In *Proceedings of the Sixth Workshop on NLP for Similar Languages, Varieties and Dialects* (pp. 42–53). Association for Computational Linguistics. https://doi.org/10.18653/v1/W19-1405.

Dunn, J. (2020). Mapping languages: The Corpus of Global Language Use. *Language Resources and Evaluation*, *54*, 999–1018. https://doi.org/10.1007/s10579-020-09489-2.

Dunn, J. (2022a). Exposure and emergence in usage-based grammar: Computational experiments in 35 languages. *Cognitive Linguistics*, *33*(4), 659–699.

Dunn, J. (2022b). *Natural language processing for corpus linguistics*. Cambridge University Press.

Dunn, J. (2023a). Syntactic variation across the grammar: Modelling a complex adaptive system. *Frontiers in Complex Systems, 1.* https://doi.org/10.3389/fcpxs.2023.1273741.

Dunn, J. (2023b). Variation and instability in dialect-based embedding spaces. In *Tenth Workshop on NLP for Similar Languages, Varieties and Dialects (VarDial 2023)* (pp. 67–77). Dubrovnik, Croatia. Association for Computational Linguistics. https://doi.org/10.18653/v1/2023.vardial-1.7.

Dunn, J., Li, H., & Sastre, D. (2022). Predicting embedding reliability in low-resource settings using corpus similarity measures. In *Proceedings of the Thirteenth Language Resources and Evaluation Conference* (pp. 6461–6470). Marseille, France. European Language Resources Association. https://aclanthology.org/2022.lrec-1.693.

Dunn, J., & Nini, A. (2021). Production vs perception: The role of individuality in usage-based grammar induction. In *Proceedings of the Workshop on Cognitive Modeling and Computational Linguistics* (pp. 149–159). Association for Computational Linguistics.

Dunn, J., & Tayyar Madabushi, H. (2021). Learned construction grammars converge across registers given increased exposure. In *Conference on Natural Language Learning* (pp. 268–278). Association for Computational Linguistics.

Dunn, J., & Wong, S. (2022). Stability of syntactic dialect classification over space and time. In *Proceedings of the 29th International Conference on Computational Linguistics* (pp. 26–36). Gyeongju, Republic of Korea. International Committee on Computational Linguistics. https://aclanthology.org/2022.lrec-1.693.

Ellis, N. (2007). Language acquisition as rational contingency learning. *Applied Linguistics, 27*(1), 1–24.

Fodor, J. D., & Crowther, C. (2002). Understanding stimulus poverty arguments. *The Linguistic Review, 19*(1–2), 105–145. https://doi.org/10.1515/tlir.19.1-2.105.

Gazdar, G., Klein, E. H., Pullum, G. K., & Sag, I. A. (1985). *Generalized phrase structure grammar*. Blackwell.

Goldberg, A. (1995). *Constructions: A construction grammar approach to argument structure*. Chicago University Press.

Goldberg, A. (2006). *Constructions at work: The nature of generalization in language*. Oxford University Press.

Goldberg, A. (2019). *Explain me this: Creativity, competition, and the partial productivity of constructions*. Princeton University Press.

Goldsmith, J. (2001). Unsupervised learning of the morphology of a natural language. *Computational Linguistics, 27*(2), 153–198.

Goldsmith, J. (2006). An algorithm for the unsupervised learning of morphology. *Natural Language Engineering, 12*(4), 353–371.

Goldsmith, J. (2015). Towards a new empiricism for linguistics. In N. Chater, A. Clark, J. Goldsmith, & A. Perfors (Eds.), *Empiricism and language learnability* (pp. 58–105). Oxford University Press. https://doi.org/10.1093/acprof:oso/9780198734260.003.0003.

Grave, E., Bojanowski, P., Gupta, P., Joulin, A., & Mikolov, T. (2018). Learning word vectors for 157 languages. In *Proceedings of the International Conference on Language Resources and Evaluation* (pp. 3483–3487). European Language Resources Association.

Grune, D., & Jacobs, C. J. H. (2008). *Parsing techniques: A practical guide* (2nd ed.). Springer.

Grünwald, P. (2007). *The minimum description length principle*. MIT Press.

Hellrich, J., Kampe, B., & Hahn, U. (2019). The influence of down-sampling strategies on SVD word embedding stability. In *Proceedings of the 3rd Workshop on Evaluating Vector Space Representations for NLP* (pp. 18–26). Association for Computational Linguistics.

Kesarwani, A. (2018). New York Times comments. Kaggle. www.kaggle.com/datasets/aashita/nyt-comments.

Kneser, R., & Ney, H. (1995). Improved backing-off for M-gram language modeling. In *Proceedings of the International Conference on Acoustics, Speech, and Signal Processing* (Vol. 1, pp. 181–184). IEEE. https://doi.org/10.1109/ICASSP.1995.479394.

Kohonen, O., Virpioja, S., & Lagus, K. (2010). Semi-supervised learning of concatenative morphology. In *Proceedings of the ACL Special Interest Group on Computational Morphology and Phonology* (pp. 78–86). Association for Computational Linguistics.

Kuperman, V., Stadthagen-Gonzalez, H., & Brysbaert, M. (2012). Age-of-acquisition ratings for 30,000 English words. *Behavior Research Methods, 44*, 978–990.

Lakoff, G., & Johnson, M. (1999). *Philosophy in the flesh: The embodied mind and its challenge to western thought*. Basic Books.

Langacker, R. (2008). *Cognitive grammar: A basic introduction*. Oxford University Press.

Leclercq, L., & Morin, C. (2023). No equivalence: A new principle of no synonymy. *Constructions, 15*(1). https://doi.org/10.24338/cons-535.

Levy, O., Goldberg, Y., & Dagan, I. (2015). Improving distributional similarity with lessons learned from word embeddings. *Transactions of the Association for Computational Linguistics, 3*, 211–225. https://doi.org/10.1162/tacl_a_00134.

Li, H., & Dunn, J. (2022). Corpus similarity measures remain robust across diverse languages. *Lingua, 275*, 103377.

Li, H., Dunn, J., & Nini, A. (2022). Register variation remains stable across 60 languages. *Corpus Linguistics and Linguistic Theory, 19*(3), 397–426.

Linzen, T. (2016). Issues in evaluating semantic spaces using word analogies. In *Proceedings of the 1st Workshop on Evaluating Vector-Space Representations for NLP* (pp. 13–18). Berlin, Germany: Association for Computational Linguistics. https://doi.org/10.18653/v1/W16-2503.

Lison, P., & Tiedemann, J. (2016). OpenSubtitles2016: Extracting large parallel corpora from movie and TV subtitles. In *Proceedings of the Tenth International Conference on Language Resources and Evaluation (LREC'16)* (pp. 923–929). European Language Resources Association (ELRA).

Mikolov, T., Chen, K., Corrado, G., & Dean, J. (2013). Efficient estimation of word representations in vector space. arXiv. https://doi.org/10.48550/ARXIV.1301.3781.

Mikolov, T., Sutskever, I., Chen, K., Corrado, G., & Dean, J. (2013). Distributed representations of words and phrases and their compositionality. In *Proceedings of the 26th International Conference on Neural Information Processing Systems – Volume 2* (pp. 3111–3119). Curran Associates Inc.

Miller, G. A. (1956). The magical number seven, plus or minus two: Some limits on our capacity for processing information. *Psychological Review, 63*(2), 81–97.

Nevens, J., Doumen, J., Van Eecke, P., & Beuls, K. (2022). Language acquisition through intention reading and pattern finding. In *Proceedings of the 29th International Conference on Computational Linguistics* (pp. 15–25). International Committee on Computational Linguistics.

Nirenburg, S., & Raskin, V. (2004). *Ontological semantics*. MIT Press.

Ortman, M. (2018). Wikipedia sentences. Kaggle. https://www.kaggle.com/datasets/mikeortman/wikipedia-sentences.

Perek, F., & Patten, A. L. (2019). Towards an English constructicon using patterns and frames. *International Journal of Corpus Linguistics, 24*(3), 354–384. https://doi.org/10.1075/ijcl.00016.per.

Piao, S., Bianchi, F., Dayrell, C., D'egidio, A., & Rayson, P. (2015). Development of the multilingual semantic annotation system. In *Proceedings of the 2015 Conference of the North American Chapter of the Association for Computational Linguistics: Human Language Technologies* (pp. 1268–1274). Association for Computational Linguistics.

Rae, J. W., Potapenko, A., Jayakumar, S. M., & Lillicrap, T. P. (2019). Compressive transformers for long-range sequence modelling. arXiv. https://doi.org/10.48550/ARXIV.1911.05507.

Rousseeuw, P. (1987). Silhouettes: A graphical aid to the interpretation and validation of cluster analysis. *Computational and Applied Mathematics, 20*, 53–65.

Schler, J., Koppel, M., Argamon, S., & Pennebaker, J. (2006). Effects of age and gender on blogging. In *Proceedings of 2006 AAAI Spring Symposium on Computational Approaches for Analyzing Weblogs*. Association for the Advancement of Artificial Intelligence.

Schubert, E., & Lenssen, L. (2022). Fast k-medoids clustering in Rust and Python. *Journal of Open Source Software*, *7*(75), 4183.

Sullivan, K. (2013). *Frames and constructions in metaphoric language*. John Benjamins.

Taylor, J. (2004). *Linguistic categorization* (3rd ed.). Oxford University Press.

Tiedemann, J. (2012). Parallel data, tools and interfaces in OPUS. In *Proceedings of the Eighth International Conference on Language Resources and Evaluation (LREC'12)* (pp. 2214–2218). European Language Resources Association (ELRA).

Vlach, H. (2019). Learning to remember words: Memory constraints as double-edged sword mechanisms of language development. *Child Development Perspectives*, *13*, 159–165. https://doi.org/10.1111/cdep.12337.

Vlach, H., & DeBrock, C. A. (2019). Statistics learned are statistics forgotten: Children's retention and retrieval of cross-situational word learning. *Journal of Experimental Psychology: Learning, Memory, and Cognition*, *45*, 700–711. https://doi.org/10.1037/xlm0000611.

Wible, D., & Tsao, N. (2010). StringNet as a computational resource for discovering and investigating linguistic constructions. In *Proceedings of the Workshop on Extracting and Using Constructions in Computational Linguistics* (pp. 25–31). Association for Computational Linguistics.

Wible, D., & Tsao, N.- L. (2020). Constructions and the problem of discovery: A case for the paradigmatic. *Corpus Linguistics and Linguistic Theory*, *16*(1), 67–93. https://doi.org/10.1515/cllt-2017-0008.

Zhang, X., Zhao, J., & LeCun, Y. (2015). Character-level convolutional networks for text classification. arXiv. https://doi.org/10.48550/ARXIV.1509.01626.

Acknowledgments

This work has benefited greatly from the testing and documentation work of Allie Osborne as well as from ongoing discussions with Ben Adams, Tom Coupe, Sidney Wong, and Matthew Durward. The constructional framework has been improved also by feedback from Andrea Nini and Harish Tayyar Madabushi, as well as the participants at the first Workshop on CxGs and NLP in 2023. Without the growing community of researchers working in computational Construction Grammar, this present work would not have been possible.

Data Availability Statement

A Python package replicating all computational methods discussed in this Element is available at https://github.com/jonathandunn/c2xg.
In addition, the data and results from all grammar-learning experiments are available at https://doi.org/10.17605/OSF.IO/SA6R3.
Finally, an interactive CodeOcean widget contains the code, data, and environment necessary to carry out these experiments:
https://doi.org/10.24433/CO.9944630.v1.

Cambridge Elements

Cognitive Linguistics

Sarah Duffy

Northumbria University

Sarah Duffy is Senior Lecturer in English Language and Linguistics at Northumbria University. She has published primarily on metaphor interpretation and understanding, and her forthcoming monograph for Cambridge University Press (co-authored with Michele Feist) explores *Time, Metaphor, and Language* from a cognitive science perspective. Sarah is Review Editor of the journal, *Language and Cognition*, and Vice President of the UK Cognitive Linguistics Association.

Nick Riches

Newcastle University

Nick Riches is a Senior Lecturer in Speech and Language Pathology at Newcastle University. His work has investigated language and cognitive processes in children and adolescents with autism and developmental language disorders, and he is particularly interested in usage-based accounts of these populations.

Editorial Board

About the Series

Cambridge Elements in Cognitive Linguistics aims to extend the theoretical and methodological boundaries of cognitive linguistics. It will advance and develop established areas of research in the discipline, as well as address areas where it has not traditionally been explored and areas where it has yet to become well-established.

Cambridge Elements

Cognitive Linguistics

Elements in the Series

Language Change and Cognitive Linguistics: Case Studies from the History of Russian
Tore Nesset

Navigating the Realities of Metaphor and Psychotherapy Research
Dennis Tay

The Many Faces of Creativity: Exploring Synaesthesia through a Metaphorical Lens
Sarah Turner and Jeannette Littlemore

Metaphor, Metonymy, the Body and the Environment: An Exploration of the Factors That Shape Emotion-Colour Associations and Their Variation across Cultures
Jeannette Littlemore, Marianna Bolognesi, Nina Julich-Warpakowski, Chung-hong Danny Leung and Paula Pérez Sobrino

Applied Cognitive Linguistics and L2 Instruction
Reyes Llopis-García

Cognitive Linguistics and Language Evolution
Michael Pleyer and Stefan Hartmann

Computational Construction Grammar: A Usage-Based Approach
Jonathan Dunn

A full series listing is available at: www.cambridge.org/ECOG

Printed in the United States
by Baker & Taylor Publisher Services